THE CONSTITUTION AND CONSTITUTIONAL CHANGE IN IRELAND

Basil Chubb

Institute of Public Administration
Dublin

Published by
Institute of Public Administration
59 Lansdowne Road
Dublin 4
Ireland

ISBN 0 902173 85 5

First published as 'The Constitution of Ireland' 1963
Second Edition 1966
Third Edition 1970
Rewritten with new material 1978
Reprinted 1982
Reprinted 1985
Reprinted 1988

Set 10/11 Baskerville and printed in Ireland
by Leinster Leader Ltd., Naas, Co. Kildare

CONTENTS

ACKNOWLEDGEMENT

I am grateful to my colleagues in the School of Law at Trinity College, Dublin for helping me with many matters of law: in particular, I thank Kader Asmal and Robert Heuston. Where I have erred, it is in spite of them.

INTRODUCTION

'Constitutions define and thereby limit public power.'[1] As political institutions they came into use when the politically dominant in a number of developing Western communities felt the need to define and delimit government, and when they and their governments were prepared to abide by the law and to accord special status to particular rules of law regarded as basic.

To define and delimit public power in this way makes necessary a process of formulation and formalization. This suggests almost inevitably a document that has the force of law and, more than that, a special status among rules of law, whether legally or by convention. As K. C. Wheare says in his *Modern Constitutions,* 'The constitution, for most countries in the world, is a selection of the legal rules which govern the government of that country and which have been embodied in a document.'[2] It is in this sense that the word is used in Ireland, and in this sense that Ireland, like almost every other state except the United Kingdom, has a constitution, Bunreacht na hÉireann (the Constitution of Ireland), enacted in 1937. Also, as is the case in many, though not all, countries, the Constitution of Ireland has a higher legal status than other laws. It cannot be changed in the manner of ordinary legislation and it is regarded as having greater authority than other legal rules. It is in fact a basic document of government, a point or source of reference, an instrument by which the Government itself can be controlled. A constitution of this sort together with an independent judiciary endowed with the power to review and interpret comprise an essential combination of institutions for the safety and well-being of a liberal-democratic state. The Constitution is, therefore, a necessary object of study in order to understand Irish government and politics. A word of caution is, however, necessary. As Wheare says, a constitution contains only 'a selection' of the rules which establish and regulate government. Moreover, 'this selection does not operate in isolation. It is part of the whole system of government or constitutional structure of the country.'[3] This system comprises, in addition to the constitution itself, not only formal laws passed by the legislature in the ordinary way, but other legal rules, as well as non-legal rules and conventions which, though they have no formal status, are nevertheless effective in controlling the operation of government. If we are to get a full and accurate picture of a government, we need to study not only the constitution, but also matters to do with the structure and competence of the various organs of government which are regulated by ordinary law such as, for example, the electoral system or the allocation of functions to administrative organizations. We need also to notice the existence of practices and organizations, including important organizations such as political parties, which are not mentioned in the constitution.

A constitution is, then, only a part, albeit a vital part of the institutional framework of government. It is an even smaller part of the total political system which, besides formal institutions, includes political processes, practices and behaviour that are not expressed through formal organizations at all. Unless a country is ruled by force by an alien state with no regard for the values of the colonial people, its political system will reflect the political standards and beliefs of the inhabitants – their 'political culture' as it is termed – or at least those of the dominant group. Thus, a constitution might well be an important source of information about the political culture of its makers and those whom they represent. Going further, one might judge a constitution at any point in time by the extent to which it reflects the political culture of the people as a whole at that time. 'In so far as [it does] and written constitutional charters set forth the accepted moral standards, customs and public opinion, they themselves constitute a political force of great influence.'[4]

Even in countries with what we might term 'congruent' constitutions and whose governments and people respect them, the passage of time, changes in the pattern of social and political life, changing ideas of what public authorities should be responsible for, and new views of the proper balance between the liberty an individual may claim and the demands society may make upon him, all lead to the original wording ceasing to fit as well as it did. In such circumstances, new meanings may be read into the written words, and the most rigid phrasing of the authors may be stretched to meet situations which they never dreamed of. The experience of the United States provides a good example of this. It is for this reason that provision needs to be made for constitutional development by way of judicial interpretation on the one hand, and formal amendment on the other.

As it happens, Bunreacht na hÉireann, which dates from 1937, did – and to a considerable extent still does – reflect quite well the political culture of the vast majority of the people of the twenty-six counties. In it one can clearly detect major features of that culture, notably the great legacy of the British that both geography and history made inevitable; nationalism (for it was enacted only sixteen years after the Treaty that gave the country its independence and bequeathed it its major problem, the border); and the Catholic social teaching of the inter-war period which a ninety-three per cent Catholic population were conditioned to accept without question. Because it was a congruent constitution in the context of the twenty-six counties, it has been a political force for order and stability. That congruence, however, itself meant that it was not suitable for the peoples of Ireland as a whole and it thus constituted a barrier to whatever chance of unity there was. Today, forty years and another civil war on, many recognize this and look for changes. Even for the people of the Republic the 'fit' is less good than it was and increasingly, on this count also, changes are canvassed.

Even in the best, i.e. most 'congruent', constitutions – those which give a comparatively clear and accurate picture of the governmental system and a fair idea of the aims which governments pursue and of the limits within which they do, in practice, operate – some matters are liable to be inadequately expressed. As Wheare puts it, 'what a constitution says is one thing and what actually happens in practice may be quite another.'[5] Bunreacht na hÉireann is no exception. Such an important matter as the functions of the Government is inadequately dealt with and no one without a knowledge of Irish constitutional history could understand Article 29.4.2°. Nor would one imagine from reading the Constitution that the Oireachtas (Parliament) could today enact any law it wishes, however repugnant to the provisions of the Constitution, provided that such law is expressed to be for the purpose of securing the public safety. Yet it has been able to do so ever since 1939 by the simple expedient of retaining in being a state of national emergency, first declared in the first days of the second world war, continued for over thirty years after the end of that war and ended only to be replaced immediately by another.[6] Thus, although a study of the Constitution is without doubt important for an understanding of the government and politics of the country, it takes us only a certain distance towards such understanding.

PART ONE
Previous Constitutions

Chapter 1

THE CONSTITUTION OF DÁIL ÉIREANN

Many, perhaps most, constitutions are made at the beginning of a state's existence or at a fresh beginning. They mark the coming into being of a new state following independence or separation, or they signify a radical change or revolution. Bunreacht na hÉireann (the Constitution of Ireland), 1937, is not one of these: rather, its enactment marked an important stage in the evolution of the state.

To understand the Constitution, both the occasion for it and its contents, it is perhaps most useful to see it as the successor of two previous constitutions, the Constitution of Dáil Éireann (1919) and the Constitution of the Irish Free State (1922). The first, the Constitution of Dáil Éireann,[1] was the constitution of a would-be government, itself an arm of an independence movement. As such it was short and simple and hardly intended to provide an adequate basic law for an effective sovereign state. The second, the Constitution of the Irish Free State, was the outcome of the success, albeit qualified success, of the independence movement and it marked the full emergence of the state. It was intended to be, and was, the basic law of a new sovereign state; but it embodied arrangements demanded by the British Government and was, so many thought, merely the best that was possible in the circumstances. When the circumstances altered, changes were to be expected. Nevertheless, all three constitutions were the products of the same general movement and each succeeding effort reflects continuity and development as much as revision and alteration, evolution as much as, indeed more than, revolution.

Continuity is evident not only between these three constitutions themselves, but also between Ireland as part of the United Kingdom and as an independent state. As Brian Farrell has argued, 'Irish political culture was already developed into an established and sturdy parliamentary mould prior to political independence.'[2] The independence movement sought a take-over not a revolution. Many, in fact most, of those who led it were fighting for political freedom not revolutionary social change. 'The political, constitution and legal underpinnings were nurtured as carefully, perhaps more carefully, than the demands and occasional local claims of fighting men in the field.'[3]

That said, however, it must be recognized that the elected Sinn Féin candidates at the (British) general election of December 1918, who met in Dublin on 21 January 1919, and constituted themselves Dáil Éireann were in rebellion. They neither needed, nor had the time, to produce an elaborately fashioned or sophisticated constitution. The document was drafted in English by a committee appointed at a secret meeting of the elected Sinn Féin members on 7 January 1919. The committee consisted of George Gavan Duffy, James O'Mara, Seán T. Ó Ceallaigh, E. J. Duggan, Piaras Béaslaí and Eoin MacNeill. Its five articles were short and to the point. They covered the competence of the Dáil, the appointment and position of a prime minister and a government, the appointment of a chairman of the Dáil, the provision and audit of funds, and amendment. A 'Declaration of Independence' and a 'Democratic Programme', which though not literally part of the Constitution should be read with it, reaffirmed and elaborated what was contained in the Proclamation of the Irish Republic' of Easter 1916.

Some features of these documents should be noticed particularly for they are significant in the constitutional development of the state. The Constitution reflected the essentially democratic and republican nature of the independence movement. True, it made no mention of a republic and was, indeed, entitled 'The Constitution of Dáil Éireann'; true also – and strangely – there was no provision for a president to represent the state and act as head of state, the symbol, one might think, of a republic, as the king is of a monarchy. In general, though, it was clear enough that this was intended to be a provisional constitution for the republic for which these representatives were contending, which, as an assembly, they held they embodied, and which they hoped to make a reality.

The general pattern of government envisaged was cabinet government in the British style, for, though they were in rebellion – in the case of some of them armed rebellion – 'the founders of the new state were constitutionalists within a strongly developed parliamentary tradition.'[4] In the British manner, ministers were endowed with substantial powers for the exercise of which they were clearly to be held responsible. There was, however, a difference of emphasis in one respect. The names of ministers had to be submitted individually to the Dáil for approval, and provision was specifically made for the removal of individual ministers. Collective responsibility, as it had developed by this time in the United Kingdom with well-disciplined parties and cabinet hegemony over parliament, was, to judge by these provisions, not what the founding fathers envisaged. This desire to tilt the system more towards *parliamentary* government was evident on occasions in the subsequent proceedings of Dáil Éireann itself[5] and later in the making of the Irish Free State Constitution. Nevertheless, in general during the period 1919-22 'the Cabinet controlled the Dáil. It had a secure majority, no organized opposition and the advantage of a war situation to stimulate consensus.'[6]

The *Democratic Programme* was a statement of social and economic aims prepared by Seán T. Ó Ceallaigh who incorporated proposals made by Tom Johnson, then Treasurer of the Labour Party, and Harry Boland. It had its origins in the acceptance by Sinn Féin deputies preparing for the meeting of Dáil Éireann of 'a document drafted by the Irish Workers Delegation of the International Conference at Berne'.[7] There were other influences too, for it 'reiterated in Lalor's and Pearse's characteristic phrasing the doctrine that "the nation's sovereignty extends not only to all its citizens, but to all its natural possessions, the natural wealth-producing processes", the rights of private property to be subordinated to the public welfare'.[8] It proceeded thence to enunciate a declaration of fundamental rights and duties reflecting a lively concern for education, social welfare and equality and placing on the state responsibility for the 'development of the nation's resources . . . in the interests of and for the benefit of the Irish people', for 'the recreation and invigoration of our industries . . . on the most beneficial and progressive co-operative and industrial lines', and for international co-operation to secure 'a general and lasting improvement in the conditions under which the working classes live and labour.'

The *Democratic Programme* no doubt incorporated basic principles of Sinn Féin: obviously also in early twentieth century terms it had a strong socialist flavour. According to Erhard Rumpf some parts of the document 'would probably not have been accepted had Griffith and de Valera been present'[9] and Piaras Béaslaí, who himself played a leading role at the time and was present, doubts 'whether a majority of the members would have voted for it, without amendment, had there been any immediate prospect of putting it into force.' He adds: 'if any charge of insincerity could be made against the first Dáil, it would be on this score.'[10] More charitably, and probably rightly, Rumpf says that those 'who at this inspired moment approved with acclamation everything that was put to them, afterwards hardly knew what had actually been in the documents.'[11] In Farrell's view, 'this was another political manoeuvre designed to win support.'[12]

Subsequent chapters will show that those features of Ireland's first constitution that were congruent with the culture would become established. Republicanism was to triumph, though not without difficulties and hesitations. What socialism there was in the independence movement was quickly to be dissipated and replaced by Catholic principles. A British-type cabinet system was to become firmly established as tentative moves towards parliamentary government failed and the Dáil took its place as a somewhat puny legislature, a victim to the lusty vigour of the cabinet. Some of these developments were, however, at first masked and deflected by the second of Ireland's constitutions, a constitution not wholly of her own making.

Chapter 2

THE CONSTITUTION OF THE IRISH FREE STATE

The Constitution of the Irish Free State reflected the occasion and the circumstances of its making.[1] It was 'the organic law of a new state'.[2] A new entity in the world of sovereign states had come into being, was operating and was recognized. The Irish Free State was one of a number of new states in Europe which had arisen out of the wars and revolutions of the time and its government was thus one among many who were constitution-making at this time. There was, however, one important difference. Though the occasion of the Constitution was the success of the independence movement, the relationship of Ireland and Britain was still, perforce, a very special one and could not but be influenced by the history of Anglo-Irish relations and by British constitutional ideas and patterns.

The combination of these two circumstances, independence on the one hand and a unique connection on the other, provided the makings of contradictions and struggle. The struggle is to be seen in the civil war and the subsequent political history of Ireland. The contradictions are apparent in the Constitution itself. On the one hand, 'it had the characteristic dogmatic ring of all constitutions which embody not the legislative crystallization of an organic development, but the theoretical postulates of a revolutionary upheaval.'[3] On the other hand, it embodied important British political concepts like the commonwealth principle and retained its archaic symbols, which were the product of a political tradition that abhorred close definition or statements of fundamentals of any kind.

Although for many this Constitution did not go far enough, it was 'the most revolutionary constitutional project in the political history of the two islands since the instruments of government of the Cromwellian period', for it was essentially republican.[4] 'It is ... perfectly clear', wrote Hugh Kennedy, first Attorney General of the Irish Free State, 'that fundamental sovereign authority proceeds from the people in the first instance to the elected representatives of Ireland in Dáil Éireann assembled'.[5] The 'undoubted right' which the Constituent Assembly asserted that it had to enact the Constitution was explicitly stated to come 'from God to the people'. Reiterating this, Article 2 of the Constitution declared that 'all powers of government and all authority, legislative, executive and judicial in Ireland, are derived from the people in Ireland.'

This insistence on the sovereignty of the people did not arise solely from a desire to refute the British view that, as in other Commonwealth countries, the source of political authority lay in the United Kingdom. There was also apparent a desire on the part of the constitution-makers to stress the position and role of the people as opposed to the Oireachtas (parliament), and, in turn, of the Oireachtas, as the spokesman of the people, as opposed to that of the Executive Council (cabinet). This can be seen in the provisions for referendum, for the initiative, for judicial review of the Constitution, for proportional representation (which some hoped would inhibit strong parties and thus, it was thought, automatic parliamentary majorities), and in the rules about the calling and dissolution of the Oireachtas and the appointment of ministers. In fact, however, the members of the Constitution Committee charged with preparing a draft for the consideration of the Government differed one with another in the course of their work on these matters, as perhaps also did members of the Government themselves.[6]

Insofar as the dogmatic assertions of popular sovereignty were intended to exclude a British source, they were, of course, out of keeping with British and Commonwealth traditions. The Constitution was intended, by Irish leaders at least, to mark a break. However, this break was obscured to some extent (as indeed to some eyes was also the de facto sovereignty of the state) by the inclusion in the statute enacting the Constitution of a clause providing that if anything in the Constitution was repugnant to the terms of the Treaty between the United Kingdom and the newly emerged Irish Free State, it would be inoperative; by the status of the country as a member of the British Commonwealth; and by the inclusion, at British insistence and at the price of a final break between the two groups of leaders, of the symbols and institutions of government then considered appropriate for a Commonwealth country. The Irish Free State was to be 'a co-equal member' of the Commonwealth and, accordingly, 'the formalism of the British monarchial system was maintained in its full archaic tenor.'[7] Provision was made for a representative of the Crown, called Governor General, and for an oath of loyalty. The enunciation of the institutions and procedures of government followed the traditional pattern and perpetuated the traditional constitutional fictions. This concept of government and the consequential legal framework of government, formal fictions though they were, were in sharp contrast to the republican principle of Article 2. 'The result of the amalgamation was an inorganic construction inspired by tendencies diametrically opposed to each other.'[8] It had other more tragic consequences too.

Just as declarations of popular sovereignty were out of keeping with British traditions and Commonwealth practice, so too were declarations of rights and social principles. Yet most constitutions, following the American and French examples, do include such declarations. Moreover, in the Irish case, the independence movement had always in the past had a strong social conscience, as is evidenced by the inclusion of social as well as national aims in its public declarations. Attention has already been drawn to the fact that a *Democratic Programme* was adopted by the Dáil in 1919 together with its Constitution. Furthermore, a declaration of rights is intended to be a restraint upon governments, and a people imbued with liberal values would expect such an enunciation just as they would those other essential adjuncts of limited government an independent judiciary (Article 68) and a provision for judicial review of legislation to test its validity 'having regard to the provisions of the Constitution' (Article 65).

The rights which were guaranteed and protected in this way included personal rights such as habeas corpus, free expression, freedom to practise any religion, freedom of association and the inviolability of the citizen's home. These reflected in their content and tone the liberal tradition and, on the whole, British legal concepts. Further, the state was prohibited from endowing any religion, from imposing any discrimination or disability on account of religious belief and from acquiring church property by compulsion, except for certain enumerated public works and then only on payment of compensation. These provisions, together with others which we shall mention, were intended to allay the fears of Protestants.

In addition, two positive social principles were enunciated, the right of all citizens to free elementary education and the declaration that all the natural resources of the country belonged to the state. Although the latter provision (Article 11) was widely enough drawn to make full-scale nationalization possible, the rights of 1922 marked a distinct retreat from the socialist-sounding declarations of 1919. In 1922, radicals and socialists were not among those who came to power. The leaders of the country were obviously conservative in their social attitudes. Thus, with the two exceptions mentioned, the rights in this Constitution have a traditional liberal democratic ring. In content and tone they contrast markedly with the extensive declarations to be found in some contemporary constitutions such as the German (Weimar Republic) Constitution of 1919. At the same time, the Free State Constitution was not obviously influenced by Christian, much less specifically Roman Catholic, social theories. Indeed, in its insistence on non-endowment and religious equality, it leaned rather to secular indifference, but there were, as we have explained, good reasons for this in the circumstances.

The system of government for which provision was made followed in the main the British pattern. However, following the proposals of the drafting committee, an attempt was made to correct what were regarded as the imperfections of that system by including devices and procedures to prevent strong cabinets backed by big and well-disciplined parties from establishing a hegemony over government. On the one hand, therefore, there was 'a bold attempt to capture the essential elements of cabinet government and squeeze them into the phraseology of constitutional clauses'[9] which went far beyond that of the Dáil Constitution. On the other hand, the provisions for the referendum, the initiative, and the novel 'extern minister' system, together with rules clearly intended to increase the role of the Oireachtas, all reflected a desire to modify the system as it worked in practice in the United Kingdom. The confidence in the ability of constitutional devices to do this, in the event turned out to be unjustified. In any case, some of those in power never desired or expected anything but strong cabinet government. Certainly, in those dangerous first days of the new state, that was very much the order of the day.

Equally in error were the views expressed during the Dáil debates that large parties and strong party discipline would not develop in Ireland. Vain, also, were the hopes of the proponents of the 'extern minister' device which, when it was first mooted, was thought to be a way of bringing the dissident de Valera and his anti-Treaty colleagues into government.[10] The split over the Treaty had effectively polarized Irish politics – as it turned out, for generations.

The influence of political events and the exigencies of governing led to the Irish Free State Constitution being much amended. No fewer than twenty-seven amending acts were passed. Until 1932, most of the changes were concerned with the reform of the Senate or the removal of those devices which had been grafted on to the cabinet system (initiative, referendum, extern ministers) and had not 'taken'. In the mid-twenties cabinet committees were at work reviewing the Constitution systematically and suggesting changes both of detail and of substance. The judges were also asked if they had any observations on suggested changes.[11] Although the changes made included important alterations in the machinery of government, they did not indicate dissatisfaction with the cabinet system in general; in fact rather the reverse, for they reflected a tendency to accept that system in its 'undiluted' form, a tendency that became more marked with the coming to office of de Valera in 1932.

Although the Cumann na nGaedheal leaders who were in office in the first decade of independence were prepared to tinker with the machinery of government as necessity, convenience or experience dictated, in respect of Commonwealth status and all that went with it, they felt bound by the Treaty and the Constitution as originally enacted. They did, nevertheless, seek at successive imperial conferences (meetings of leaders of Commonwealth countries) 'a loosening of the fabric of the Commonwealth' itself.[12] Their policy was, thus, as Mansergh put it, 'to refashion the Commonwealth in closer accord with Irish interests and outlook': in contrast, that of Fianna Fáil was 'to seek the first opportunity to unravel or by one dramatic revolutionary stroke to sever Irish ties with the Commonwealth.'[13] One way or another a radical revision was inevitable after de Valera assumed office.

This revision involved, at first, the removal from the Constitution by amendment of the symbols and procedures of the Commonwealth – and the amendments from 1932 onwards were mainly concerned with this – and, then, the making of an entirely new constitution, 'new from top to bottom' and 'unquestionably indigenous in character'.[14] The new Constitution would stress more strongly the republican nature of the state and would replace Commonwealth status by a looser form of association. To do this meant, of course, repudiating the Treaty.

PART TWO
Bunreacht na hÉireann

Chapter 3

THE INTERNATIONAL STATUS OF THE STATE

Constitutions reflect the principles and interests of those who make them or some compromise or conflation of opposing principles and interests. If the Irish Free State Constitution was of the latter variety Bunreacht na hÉireann (the Constitution of Ireland) was to a large extent of the former, for it was in a very real sense de Valera's Constitution.[1] In the course of the debates on it, he made it clear that, though its principles had been agreed to 'after a number of Government discussions', he had personally drafted it, consulting and taking advice from officials and others, including a number of Catholic clergy, some of whom prepared papers and drafts for him.[2] He presented it to the people (in a radio broadcast) and to the Dáil and, virtually single-handed, he piloted it through its various stages, explaining and defending it with all an author's intimate knowledge of, and love for, his work. It is possible, therefore, to get from the Dáil Debates of May and June 1937, a very clear picture both of the basic principles on which the Constitution rests and of the arguments for this or that particular provision or wording as put by their author. We do not need to speculate in this case as to what a group of founding fathers had in their minds or could have meant: to a large extent we know.

Since it was over the relationship of Ireland to Great Britain and the Commonwealth that de Valera and his supporters had parted company from the 'Pro-Treaty' Party, it is natural that Bunreacht na hÉireann should mark a distinct alteration in Irish law in that relationship and in Ireland's status. As we have observed, the Irish

Free State Constitution had embedded in it 'the conflicting constitutional doctrines of the British monarchical system and Irish Republicanism'.[3] This conflict was now resolved formally, though not without some last vestiges of equivocation, as we shall see. The new arrangements were designed to vindicate de Valera's stand over the years and to make it seem that the state had now won a freedom not achieved under the first – 'Pro-Treaty' – government. In general, de Valera's view of the matter probably reflected that of most Irish people. Another stage in the evolution of the Irish State had been completed, it seemed, save for some tidying up that had to wait another decade. To have achieved what was now being enacted – and subsequently to have taken up and successfully maintained a neutral stance during the second world war – finally persuaded people that the state was indeed a sovereign state.

Bunreacht na hÉireann contains a restatement of the Irish republican position, unqualified by British constitutional theory or Commonwealth symbolism. The basis of all governmental authority, including the authority to enact the Constitution, is clearly stated to be the people. The Constitution was *proposed* by the Government, *approved* by the Dáil, but *enacted* by the people. As de Valera told his radio audience when he introduced his Constitution to them, 'sovereignty resides in them the people as their inalienable and indefeasible right.' They had the right to give themselves a new basic law and only they had that right. Accordingly, the Preamble states: 'We, the people of Éire . . . do hereby adopt, enact, and give to ourselves this Constitution.' The phrase 'we, the people of Éire' follows that first used by the United States which, in one form or another, is found in many modern constitutions. It symbolizes the desire to have explicit recognition of the political theory that lay behind its use in 1789. Nor are these mere declamatory flourishes; they are accepted law, for the courts speak of the Constitution as having been enacted by the people,[4] and proposed amendments to it require the approval of the electorate at a referendum.[5]

'The people of Éire' referred to are, of course, the people of the whole island of Ireland, as Article 2 makes clear. However, the use here of 'Éire' – the Irish word for Ireland – which reflected de Valera's desire to have Irish used wherever possible, did have the unfortunate consequence of obscuring that claim somewhat.[6] The state became widely known throughout the world as Éire, a word designating the twenty-six county state that existed in practice and formerly known as the Irish Free State. Moreover, notwithstanding the claim to the full extent of what was considered to be 'the national territory', the existing situation had perforce to be recognized in fact and in the Constitution itself. Consequently, Article 3 declares that, 'pending the reintegration of the national territory', the laws of the state shall have effect over the same area as hitherto i.e. over the twenty-six counties.

The people, though they may be recognized as the source of authority in fact, are a law-giver unknown to British law; and this clear constitutional expression of popular sovereignty – a denial of rule from without and an assertion of the right to make the most fundamental laws within – destroyed the state's Commonwealth status and was intended to do so. In this sense it could be said in truth that Bunreacht na hÉireann marked a new beginning. We have argued, however, that Ireland's constitutions are best seen as milestones in an evolution or development, and this is well confirmed by the failure of Bunreacht na hÉireann to declare the state formally a republic. For some people, in fact, the failure to do this was 'the most surprising thing about these provisions'.[7] Yet Article 4 declares only that 'the *name* of the state is Éire, or in the English language, Ireland' and Article 5 that 'Ireland is a sovereign, independent, democratic state.' It is clear enough, of course, that these articles, together with the provision for a President as formal head of state and the declaration of popular sovereignty, made Ireland in effect a republic. Why, then, was it not clearly stated to be so? True, that prototype of republican constitutions, the American, does not make such a declaration either, but, given the recent history of Ireland, it might have been expected that the point would be most explicitly made.

This was, nevertheless, a deliberate omission, reflecting a consistent policy, the policy of 'external association' which de Valera had steadily pursued. At the abdication of King Edward VIII in 1936, this policy had been reflected in the arrangements provided for in the Constitution (Amendment no. 27) Act and in the Executive Authority (External Relations) Act, 1936, by which the Crown had been removed from the Irish Free State Constitution and reinstated on a simple statutory basis as an instrument which might be used by the Irish state for some purposes of external relations.[8] To have declared the state formally a republic in 1937 would have involved a complete break with the Commonwealth, for the statesmen and constitutional lawyers of the time held that a monarch in common was an essential feature of Commonwealth membership, in fact its basic symbol. As de Valera and many others believed, such a declaration would have made impossible for ever the eventual inclusion of Northern Ireland in the state. De Valera made the point quite explicitly: 'If the Northern problem were not there ... in all probability there would be a flat, downright proclamation of a republic in this [the Constitution].'[9] This omission and a second equivocation, the inclusion of Article 29.4.2°, which in rather obscure language permits the continuance of the arrangements envisaged in the Executive Authority (External Relations) Act, were intended as planks for 'a bridge over which the Northern Unionists might one day walk.'[10]

These articles on the status of the state and the source of political authority stated the position as it already existed in the Irish view. They were, said de Valera, 'giving a power which has been clearly and obviously suggested by the exact circumstances in which we find ourselves at the moment.' His version had another advantage in his eyes: 'it puts the question of our international relations in their proper place – and that is outside the Constitution.'[11] Together, his proposals i.e. no formal declaration of a Republic and the continuance on a permissive basis of the External Relations Act, would, he pointed out, allow for easy evolution, since not one word of the Constitution would have to be changed to break the link or to declare the state formally a republic, if and when it became advantageous to do so. He was quite right. When, in 1948, John A. Costello's Coalition Government did decide to do so, no constitutional amendment was necessary. It was sufficient to repeal the External Relations Act, to assign all executive powers in connection with external affairs to the President acting on the advice of the Government, and to declare that 'the description of the state shall be the Republic of Ireland', all of which were done by the Republic of Ireland Act, 1948.[12] With this Act, the position was finally tidied up.

The breaking of this tenuous link on Easter Day 1949 at last brought a formal acknowledgement by the United Kingdom and the Commonwealth countries that Ireland was, indeed, no longer a member of the Commonwealth.[13] That they had not formally recognized the change occasioned by the enacting of the Constitution in 1937 but, on the contrary, had declared that they saw no fundamental alteration, did not alter the fact that, from that date, Ireland regarded herself, and was widely regarded, as being no longer a member of the Commonwealth. As Mansergh has pointed out, to have taken up a formalistic attitude of no change, as the Commonwealth countries did, was probably unwise, for this was to miss a second chance – the first was in 1921 – of recognizing that Commonwealth status was not suited to Ireland. It caused 'a notable difference of view between the Irish government and the governments of the Commonwealth about the status of Éire' to exist for twelve years.[14]

While it may be thought curious that a matter as fundamental as the nature of the state should be deliberately omitted from the Constitution, the policy embodied in the External Relations Act and Bunreacht na hÉireann was, as Mansergh argued, the first attempt to explore the possibility of establishing an intimate relationship between a republic and the British Commonwealth, 'the symbol of whose free association was the Crown.'[15] At the very time when the Republic of Ireland Act was enacted and the opportunity of exploring these possibilities further in an Irish context was extinguished, they were being actively pursued – and with success – by other states newly emerging from British control.

To this day, Ireland is not, and hardly could be, regarded as a completely foreign state in the United Kingdom. Under the Ireland Act, the Republic of Ireland, as the state was to be known in the United Kingdom, 'was not to be a foreign country, and the provisions of the British Nationality Act, 1948, defining aliens in such a manner as to exclude citizens of Éire, was made applicable to citizens of the Republic of Ireland.' Also, the chief diplomatic representative of the Republic of Ireland in London was to have 'the same diplomatic privileges as are given to Commonwealth High Commissioners.'[16] Thus, the close association of the two countries was confirmed, as in so many ways continues to be the case.

Chapter 4

THE SOVEREIGNTY OF THE PEOPLE AND THE ROLE OF THE PRESIDENT

Just as Bunreacht na hÉireann asserts *national* sovereignty so, too, it stresses *popular* sovereignty. In the role it assigns to the people, however, it by no means follows its predecessor.

The Constitution of the Irish Free State provided comparatively liberally for popular and parliamentary participation, though it sullied the theoretical purity of the concept of popular sovereignty by the inclusion of the Crown as the source of power. Bunreacht na hÉireann, on the other hand, envisages more meagre provision for popular participation while proclaiming the sovereignty of the people, qualified only by a Christian recognition that all authority comes from God. The state is declared to be 'democratic' and it is explicitly stated in Article 6 that 'all powers of government, legislative, executive and judicial, derive, *under God,* from the people, whose right it is to designate the rulers of the state and, in final appeal, to decide all questions of national policy, *according to the requirements of the common good*.' The qualifications (italicized by the author) are important. 'Popular sovereignty, absolute in one sense, is conditional in another.'[1] In this respect the Constitution goes much further than the Irish Free State Constitution which, though it proclaimed in the preamble that 'all lawful authority comes from God to the people', stated simply (in Article 2) that 'all powers of Government and all authority, legislative, executive, and judicial are derived from the people of Ireland.'

Irish republican thought, though deriving in general from American and French ideas, was never in the main stream of European liberal theory. It had on the whole never been doctrinaire or dogmatic and was now, with national independence achieved, becoming ever more qualified and modified by the influence of Catholic teaching. The Cumann na nGaedheal governments of the first decade enacted, with every appearance of public approval, measures that clearly reflected an austere Catholic approach to social problems. These included the Censorship of Films Act, 1923, the Intoxicating Liquor Acts, 1924 & 1927, the Censorship of Publications Act, 1929, and the amending of Dáil Standing Orders to exclude the use of private bill procedure to obtain a divorce.[2] In Bunreacht na hÉireann this trend was extended into the basic law of the state; in places it is markedly Roman Catholic in language and content. In his study *Church & State in Modern Ireland, 1923-1970*, John Whyte, in a chapter entitled 'The Catholic Moral Code enshrined in the Law of the State', dubbed Bunreacht na hÉireann 'the coping-stone of this development'.[3]

Since, on the other hand, the liberal principles that permeated the Irish Free State Constitution and – as we have argued – which were accepted by Irish people were by no means abandoned, de Valera's constitution was, in Mansergh's words, an attempt 'to reconcile the notion of an inalienable popular sovereignty with the older medieval notion of a theocratic state.'[4] In presenting his draft to the Dáil, de Valera had declared that 'if there is one thing more than another that is clear and shining through this whole Constitution, it is the fact that the people are the masters';[5] the language used in the Constitution, however, has a different nuance. The authority of the people is not after all absolute or unqualified; it must be exercised 'according to the requirements of the common good' and is subject to a final spiritual sanction. In a country whose political leaders at that period and for many years thereafter sometimes went out of their way to stress their respect for clerical pronouncements, such qualifications might have been of great importance. By the seventies, as we shall see, things had changed somewhat.

Abstract political philosphies notwithstanding, the stark fact is that people can play only a limited part in government. The governors they choose to rule them and the deputies to represent them, who are in theory responsible to them, might misunderstand their masters, be tempted to behave in an arbitrary way, even to try to undermine the constitution. How were de Valera's 'masters' to have their mastery assured? His answer was the office of the President.

The President of Ireland (Uachtarán na hÉireann), while he 'neither rules nor reigns', was conceived of by de Valera as not merely a formal head of state, useful and indeed essential in all states

whatever their political complexions, but as the guardian of the people's rights and of the Constitution. In de Valera's own words, 'he is there to guard the people's rights and mainly to guard the Constitution' and he is invested with certain functions and powers to do this. 'In exercising these powers he is acting on behalf of the people who have put him there for that special purpose.'[6] His link with the people is emphasized by the fact that he is directly elected. These functions, which involve the exercise of personal discretion, are an interesting and important addition to his other functions as head of state, i.e. those of acting both as the symbol of the state and the centre of ceremonial and of performing a number of formal acts of government.

Neither as the guardian of the Constitution and the people's rights thereunder nor as the head of state is the President in any sense the head of the government or the source of governmental power. The government is not 'His Excellency's' as the British government is 'Her Majesty's'; on the contrary, the head of the government is explicitly stated to be the Taoiseach (Article 28.5.1°). It is sufficient for the Taoiseach to 'keep the President generally informed on matters of domestic and international policy' (Article 28.5.2°); and, in practice, even this does not amount to much. Cosgrave, for example, is known to have visited President Ó Dálaigh on only four occasions during his two years as President.[7] Nor is there much vestige of prerogative power lying with the President as head of state, or of authority to act to save an entity called 'the state'. On the contrary, as the provision for direct election is intended to signify, he is the representative of the people, although the conniving of government and opposition parties has on four out of eight occasions produced an agreed candidate and deprived the people of choice. In this capacity, he is charged with specific duties that involve the use of his personal discretion on their behalf, duties which might entail him restraining or thwarting the government of the day or obliging the government to submit to the judgment of the people.

The President's powers of this kind – he has other discretionary powers as well – are four. First, he may refer any bill to the Supreme Court for a decision on whether it contains anything repugnant to the Constitution which, having been enacted by the sovereign people, is legally and morally superior. Up to the end of 1977, five bills had been so referred.[8] A government that wished to persist with a provision declared repugnant would have to submit it to the electorate in a referendum; thus the people would have the final say. Second, the provision under Article 27 for a referendum on proposed legislation (which is an attenuation of the provision in the Irish Free State Constitution) involves Presidential discretion. If a majority of the members of Seanad Éireann (the Senate) and not less than one-third of the members of the Dáil by joint petition request him to decline to sign a bill on the ground that it 'contains a proposal of such national importance that the will of the people thereon ought to be ascertained', he may, if he so decides, accede to the request and will then only sign if and when the proposal shall have been approved by the people at a referendum or by a resolution of a new Dáil after a dissolution and a general election. Third, the President may at any time convene a meeting of either or both houses of the Oireachtas (Parliament), a provision which is obviously intended to cover an emergency when those whose job it is to call a meeting cannot or will not.

The powers described above enable the President to call in the people or, in the last case, their elected representatives. It may seem paradoxical that the fourth, and perhaps most important, discretionary power of this sort permits the President to *refuse* a reference to the people. Under Article 28.10, a Taoiseach is required to resign from office 'on his ceasing to retain the support of a majority in Dáil Éireann unless on his advice the President dissolves Dáil Éireann', and, under Article 13.2.2°, 'the President may in his absolute discretion refuse' a dissolution in these circumstances. If he does so refuse, the Taoiseach must resign, thus giving an opportunity to the Dáil to nominate a successor. The effect of this is, of course, to *prevent* the people from making what is surely one of the most important decisions it can make, that of who is to be the government of the state; and at a juncture when it would seem particularly appropriate for them to do so. In the only two cases in which a Taoiseach, defeated on an issue which he regarded as a matter of confidence, has asked for a dissolution, he has been granted it. Michael McDunphy, formerly Secretary to the President, put the matter very conservatively when he commented that 'it must be assumed that the President would be slow to refuse a dissolution except for very adequate reasons.'[9]

In the exercise of this function, and this function only, the President may decide without reference to anyone at all if he so wishes. Before exercising any of the other discretionary powers, he is obliged to consult the Council of State, a body comprising office holders, former office holders and anyone else up to a total of seven whom the President cares to appoint. The function of this body 'is to aid and counsel the President in the exercise of certain of his duties, but the President is under no obligation to accept its advice.'[10] In practice, circumstances in which the President has to consider whether or not to exercise a discretionary function have seldom arisen and the Council has, therefore, met only infrequently. Up to the end of 1977 Presidents had summoned it on only eight occasions, on all but one of them to consult with it as to whether proposed legislation should be referred to the Supreme Court for a decision as to whether the bill or a part thereof was repugnant.

It is undeniable that these powers vested in the President are politically important and their exercise might involve him in controversy, the more so since they are to be exercised precisely at periods of political disagreement or crisis. Certainly, in the circumstances and political climate of the first two decades of the state's existence, their exercise by a President elected, as Presidents have been, on party lines, would inevitably have led to the office and the person becoming involved in political controversy. It would almost certainly not have been sufficient for a President to say that he was acting on behalf of the people who put him there for that special purpose. Indeed, when the draft Constitution was being debated, the opposition feared the worst, though their attitude was undoubtedly influenced by their anticipation of de Valera's assuming the office at that time.[11]

The reaction of the opposition on the two occasions (1938 and 1944) when a defeated Taoiseach advised, and was granted, a dissolution, suggests that it was only the continued existence of stable majorities in the Dáil and the absence of extraordinary crises that prevented the office becoming a 'political' office in the years immediately following the enactment of the Constitution. As it happened, the country had thirty-five years experience of inactive heads of state insulated from party strife, sedulous in keeping themselves outside and above political controversy, and as sedulously being excluded from affairs by political leaders. In such circumstances, the character of the office seemed to have been permanently established as the most dignified office (in Bagehot's sense of that term) imaginable; a political Trappist, silent on any matter that could conceivably be thought of as political.

The reaction of most politicians to the concept of a President who should be more active than his somewhat inert predecessors, put forward by Erskine Childers both before and after his election in 1973, suggests that they had come to expect a torpid head of state. Childers, on the contrary, believed that the President should openly espouse social causes that were incontrovertibly in the public interest and that he could appropriately speak on matters on which the parties and the public were virtually unanimous. He evoked a stirring of unease among politicians, particularly when he actually put a toe into dangerous Northern waters.[12] At once it was apparent that it would be very difficult to obtain the best of all three worlds; a non-political President, symbolizing the state and exercising mostly formal powers, who yet would actively epitomize the nation, and who in emergency or political crisis would act with unquestionable authority in the name of the people. There would almost certainly be someone to question any activities in the second and third of these capacities.

If Childers evoked warning growls by a very modest extension of the President's activities in one direction, his successor, Cearbhall Ó Dálaigh, was the subject of criticism that led directly to a constitutional crisis and his resignation when he showed signs of a more lively interest than his predecessors in another aspect of his job.[13] Paradoxically, one might think, the crisis involved a President who had had a distinguished career as a judge both in Ireland and in the European Court and a government headed by a Taoiseach who had always made much of his devotion to law and order and the preservation of the institutions of the state.

When, in September 1976, President Ó Dálaigh sought the advice of the Council of State as to whether the Emergency Powers Bill, 1976, and the Criminal Law Bill, 1976, should be referred to the Supreme Court for a decision on constitutionality and subsequently did refer the Emergency Powers Bill, he was clearly acting within his constitutional powers. It might be thought also that this was a very proper reference, for the Bill gave great powers to the authorities. Although, in the Government's view, by virtue of the provisions of Article 28.3.3° the bill was immune from being declared unconstitutional, the Oireachtas having declared a state of emergency, some doubted whether such a declaration automatically excluded the courts or whether the declaration itself was wholly immune from judicial scrutiny.[14]

As Ó Dálaigh's letter of 19 October 1976 makes clear,[15] it was on this point – whether there existed a genuine state of emergency – that he referred the bill. Although the Supreme Court found that the bill was not unconstitutional, the Chief Justice in his judgement indicated that Ó Dálaigh's view that the Court had the power to enquire into the question of the existence of a genuine state of emergency was shared by the judges. Ó Dálaigh's action in referring the question might, indeed, have reflected the view of the judiciary, or a section of it, about their role vis-à-vis the executive.

The Government, on the other hand, or at least some members of it, were privately critical of what they considered was an unjustified attempt to hold up a bill deemed by them to be necessary and perhaps urgent. It is possible that that would have been the end of the matter, however, were it not for a farcical episode in an army mess hall. In a speech at the opening of new catering facilities at Mullingar, the Minister for Defence, Patrick Donegan, a convivial and ebullient man of ‘hot and generous temperament’, referred to the powers of the gardaí and the army and continued:

> we want to defend this state and the man who wants to go to bed at night and wake up in the morning. It was amazing when the President sent the Emergency Powers Bill to the Supreme Court . . . In my opinion he is a thundering disgrace. The fact is that the army must stand behind the state.[16]

Donegan said subsequently that because of a minor car accident on the previous day, he was ‘concussed and did not know it . . . [he] was like a zombie walking around.’[17] Nevertheless, he also made it clear that he had what he thought were good reasons to be critical, and many believed that the criticism of the President was deliberate and reflected the views of a number of ministers, though everyone deplored the actual words used.

Although Donegan apologised at once and offered to resign, the Taoiseach declined the offer. Refusing the demands of the opposition to dismiss him, Cosgrave described Donegan's remarks ‘as a serious comment on what the President did, in a disrespectful way . . . There was no quesion of the Constitution being challenged.’[18] The President saw it otherwise – in failing to dismiss Donegan the Taoiseach was, in his view, standing over his statements – and he resigned, a step that some judged to be inevitable and others an overreaction. Describing the minister's remarks as ‘outrageous criticism’, Ó Dálaigh stated his views of the President's role:

> If the office of President, as I conceive it to be, is to have any usefulness, a President would be failing his duty ‘to maintain the Constitution of Ireland and uphold its laws’, if he were not vigilant in his scrutiny of legislative proposals.[19]

Vigilance of this sort, though, could clearly bring a President into political controversy, though it should not open him to abuse, let alone abuse that is shrugged off in the way that Cosgrave and his colleagues did in this case.

The dichotomy in the Presidency is obvious and John Kelly, then Parliamentary Secretary to the Taoiseach, put his finger on it when he argued in the Dáil that there is ‘a distinction between the incumbent of the office and the office itself’ and between his formal powers and his discretionary powers. The President 'must be prepared for the wind of criticism to which everybody else in public life who makes a decision is also subject.'[20] The President as head of state and first citizen should be above criticism; but if President A chooses to exercise any of the real powers given to him in the Constitution, his judgement might be questioned and he must not expect to escape criticism.

In his nomination speech Ó Dálaigh's successor, Patrick Hillery, said 'I was nominated by the [Fianna Fáil] Party to establish a principle – the constitutional position of the President.'[21] But what is that position? President Hillery was begging a very vexed question. Perhaps, as Gallagher has suggested, 'the office of the Presidency as envisaged by Mr de Valera and laid down by the Constitution is an inherently unsatisfactory one.'[22]

Chapter 5

THE MACHINERY OF GOVERNMENT

Ireland got a new Constitution in 1937 because de Valera and the Fianna Fáil Party were dissatisfied with the Constitution of the Irish Free State; but this dissatisfaction was, as we have pointed out, centred mainly on Commonwealth status and symbols. In general, the machinery of government, which was based on what might appropriately be termed the early twentieth-century Westminster model of cabinet government, was not in dispute. Far from it: the trend towards a governmental system of the British type, operating in a manner similar to the British, and unmodified by 'continental' devices, which can be seen in the constitutional amendments of the period 1922-32, was confirmed under de Valera. He found the system which he inherited an adequate instrument for his purposes and, indeed, well suited to a strong prime minister leading a loyal majority party that looked to him for initiative and direction.

Accordingly, Bunreacht na hÉireann to a large extent confirmed what already existed formally or in practice. Many of the words and phrases used were similar to those used in the previous Constitution. The device of the 'extern minister', the most novel feature of 1922, which became an unused option after 1927, disappeared altogether.[1] What modifications there were were largely intended to increase the status and powers of the prime minister (now called Taoiseach); for whereas the Irish Free State Constitution tended, if anything, to play down his role, the new Constitution pays considerable attention to him and specifically assigns duties and powers to him that were formerly assigned to the cabinet as a whole. To a large extent, however, these provisions only made formal what was in fact the practice, if not under W. T. Cosgrave before 1932, then certainly under de Valera. 'What is being done here', de Valera explained, 'has been to translate into practice what has been done in the past.' It was in fact 'only making explicit what was implicit all the time.'[2]

Although the constitutional provisions do not give a reader an adequate account of the functions and roles of the various institutions of government or an accurate picture of the conditions under which government is actually carried on, and cannot be expected to, they are not on the whole misleading except in one general respect, namely the use of the principle of a separation of functions and powers when dealing with the organs of government. Here the authors only followed the general practice of constitution makers in the early twentieth century. They devised institutions in terms of political and constitutional theories that were widely accepted in the nineteenth century and were still regarded as the norms according to which government ought to be carried on, though in practice it was not.

In line with this approach, the Constitution enumerates the standard list of governmental functions. Article 6 refers to 'all powers of government' and goes on to specify them as 'legislative, executive and judicial'. Article 15.2 states that 'the sole and exclusive power of making laws' is vested in the Oireachtas, but provides for the establishment and recognition of 'subordinate legislatures'. Article 28.2 declares that 'the executive power of the State shall . . . be exercised by or on the authority of the Government' (as the cabinet is called in the Constitution). Article 34.1 provides that 'justice shall be administered in courts established by law by judges appointed in the manner provided by this Constitution', though Article 37 modifies this for it permits the assignment of limited judicial functions to administrative tribunals.

A division of functions and powers along the lines suggested by the literal meaning of the words of the Constitution does not obtain in Ireland. It would be absurd to think of the Government as having only 'executive' functions. On the contrary, the great virtue of the cabinet system is that it provides a focus of power and responsibility in one group who are at the same time party leaders and leading members of the Oireachtas, besides being ministers. Again, it would be misleading to envisage the Oireachtas as 'making laws' in the literal sense or to the extent that American congressmen, for example, are 'legislators'. The Oireachtas has the authority to declare law and thus to legitimize it. Although it makes some contribution to its content by way of criticism and amendment, the initiative in preparing and proposing bills rests almost wholly with the government, and the origins and formulation of legislation owe little to the Oireachtas as such. Furthermore, it is universally the experience that, notwithstanding constitutional declarations of the separation of powers, the development of the modern welfare state has not only placed more and more of the onus for planning and initiation of business upon the government, but 'has given rise, on the one hand, to an increasing delegation of law-making powers to the executive, and, on the other, to the conferring of functions of adjudication upon the executive itself or upon agencies responsible to it or directly or indirectly under its control.'[3] These have 'made considerable inroads' upon this constitutional doctrine.

It is not intended to deal with the structure and working of Irish government here.[4] We need only repeat that in general the system provided for in Bunreacht na hÉireann follows the British model. There are differences, however. Because Ireland is much smaller, its governmental machinery is less complex. In fact, the government resembles the British cabinet of the turn of the century rather than the more complicated structure of today, with its considerable hierarchy of ministers and its complex of cabinet committees. Again, because of social and electoral differences, the role of the parliamentary representative differs from that of the British M.P., though not so much from that of some Commonwealth parliamentarians. Also, the Senate is very different in its composition from the House of Lords (it could hardly be otherwise) and, indeed, from any other Senate.

On the whole, however, what is notable is not the differences but the similarities in form and practice which extend not only to the Government and Government-Oireachtas relationships but to parliamentary procedure, the forms of administrative organization and the distribution of functions between them, the structure and professional standards of the civil service and, until the reforms of the early seventies in Great Britain, the structure of local government. Naturally, the passage of time increases the propensity to look elsewhere for models and analogues, as Irish horizons have gradually widened to include Northern and Western Europe. As yet though, no one looking at Irish government today could mistake its parentage.

This similarity might be thought in one respect to be strange. The foundations in constitutional theory of the two systems are, as we have shown, somewhat different. Republican declarations of popular sovereignty have no place in the British tradition and the extent to which people there might appropriately participate in political decision-making is evidently considered to be small, as was clearly shown by the agonizing that went on in 1975 about the propriety of a referendum on E.E.C. membership. In Ireland, it might have been expected that more attention would be paid to making a reality of popular participation so far as practicable.

In a conventional post first world war way, the Irish Free State Constitution did make gestures in that direction. It provided for the use of popular initiative in proposing legislation and for a referendum on legislative proposals at the request of three-fifths of the Senate or one-twentieth of the voters, together with reference of constitutional amendments to the electorate. However, successive constitutional amendments (under the Constitution, these could be made without a referendum in the first eight years) removed the initiative and the referendum altogether. Bunreacht na hÉireann restored a limited provision for a referendum on proposed legislation which up to the end of 1977 had never been used.[5] Constitutional amendments also require approval at a referendum.[6] The importance of this check was illustrated on the first occasions on which it was used. In 1959, a proposal to substitute a simple majority system for the existing proportional representation system at elections was rejected, and, in 1968, the same proposal, once again put forward by the Government and passed by the Oireachtas, was similarly – and this time decisively – defeated.

All in all, referenda on constitutional amendments plus what is the universal practice of all democracies, direct election of parliamentary and local authority representatives, are the sum total of popular participation. It is true that the Constitution does allow for, though it does not require, the development of subordinate legislatures and functional or vocational councils (Art. 15) and 'for the direct election by any functional or vocational group or association or council of so many members of Seanad Éireann as may be fixed by . . . law in substitution for an equal number of members' elected in the manner otherwise prescribed (Art. 19). Both these provisions harked back to the Irish Free State Constitution or to ideas canvassed by the members of the Constitution Comittee. Their inclusion in the 1937 Constitution reflected the lively interest being shown by Catholic writers in the thirties in vocational organization and representation following the publication of the Papal Encyclical *Quadragesimo Anno* in 1931. The hard fact was, however, that the conditions did not exist in the community that would make vocational representation practicable, and once Catholic intellectuals quietly dropped vocational organization after the second world war, these articles were doomed to remain a dead-letter.

Mass participation was not a topic of political importance in the twenties and thirties; on the contrary, the high-watermark of democracy had been reached and for the moment the tide was receding in Western Europe. Since then the trend has been rather to centralization and bureaucracy. Procedures involving direct participation used in some Swiss cantons and in the Eastern United States were regarded as interesting historical survivals rather than as examples to be followed. The more extended use of elections and referenda practised at state and local government levels in the U.S.A. made little impact upon Western Europe. Ireland, politically and culturally a conservative and later an almost stagnant society, became and has remained stuck at the partially developed stage of democracy that had been generally attained by the first world war. In the late sixties and after, participation in the context of the workplace, the universities and the church became a lively issue and voluntary community development began to attract more support. This stirring did not, however, extend to political practice – except significantly and ominously in an increase in demonstrations and marches – and as yet there has been only a modest development by way of worker participation at board level in some state-sponsored bodies. Even quite modest suggestions e.g. that a system of local government ought to be specifically provided for in the Constitution, or for a thorough-going devolution and decentralization of public business from the centre to regions and local areas, have failed to evoke the support of politicians or the interest of the public.[7]

Chapter 6

THE COURTS AND THE RIGHTS OF THE CITIZEN

It is widely held in liberal-democratic countries that the traditional institutions of adjudication, the courts, need to be independent of, and insulated from, politics in order to perform their functions properly. This is reflected in Ireland both in constitutional theory and political practice. That is not to say that judicial functions are assigned only to courts in the ordinary judicial system, for adjudicators more closely related to the administration than to the courts abound; or that the actions of the courts do not form part of the process of government. What it does mean is that efforts are made to enable the courts to function in an autonomous way in performing their duty of saying what the law is, even if this involves restraining governments themselves.

The adequate performance of this duty is an important safeguard for the citizen and on it depends the enjoyment by the citizen of the rights he is formally guaranteed in the constitution. For whether explicitly stated or not, the duty extends to interpreting the constitution:

> While it is the duty of every institution established under the authority of a Constitution and exercising powers granted by a Constitution, to keep within the limits of those powers, it is the duty of the Courts, from the nature of their function, to say what these limits are. And that is why Courts come to interpret a Constitution.[1]

Surprisingly, one might think, that prototype of democratic constitutions, the United States Constitution, does not include a specific statement to this effect, though the power was soon inferred and declared with powerful arguments by Chief Justice Marshall in the case of *Marbury* v. *Madison* in 1803. In Bunreacht na hÉireann this power is explicitly given in Article 34.3.

The Irish Free State Constitution arranged for continuity by declaring all laws in force at the coming into operation of the Constitution to be of full effect; it provided for a court system comprising courts of first instance and a court of final appeal to be called the Supreme Court, the courts of the first instance to include courts of local and limited jurisdiction and a High Court; it declared that 'all judges shall be independent in the exercise of their functions', and laid down provisions to ensure, so far as is possible by means of law, that they should be so. The High Court was invested with full jurisdiction, its power extending 'to the question of the validity of any law having regard to the provisions of the Constitution.' The Supreme Court was invested with appellate jurisdiction over decisions of the High Court both in constitutional and other cases. In 1924, the Courts of Justice Act provided for a new system of courts and, while it recast the then existing system taken over at the inception of the state, 'there was very little change in the principles involved.'[2]

The system worked well in practice. Only the provision embodied in the Irish Free State Constitution for appeal to the British Privy Council, which was a usual feature of Commonwealth constitutions, impaired its self-sufficiency. In 1933, however, such appeals were abolished by a statute of the Oireachtas. Shortly afterwards a decision of the Judicial Committee of the Privy Council itself confirmed that, under the British Statute of Westminster (1931), this Irish act was valid in British law also and that, accordingly, such appeals could no longer be made.[3]

General satisfaction with the system was evidenced by the fact that the same arrangements were continued in Bunreacht na hÉireann, the wording used being very similar to that of 1922, though the right of appeal to the Privy Council of course disappeared. Continuity was ensured, as in 1922, by Article 50 and by a number of 'Transitory Provisions' (Articles 51-63). It is necessary to point out here that these transitory provisions no longer appear in the Constitution and to explain both how this came about and why these articles are, nevertheless, of some importance, especially when we are considering the legal system. Under two of these Articles (51 and 52) all the transitory provisions articles ceased to form part of the Constitution after certain fixed dates and the articles themselves were then to be (and were) omitted from the official published texts. Consequently no sign of these interim arrangements is to be found in copies of the Constitution published after 1941. However,

Articles 52-63 continued to have the force of law where appropriate. This was a point of importance so far as the courts of law were concerned for, until the enactment of the Courts (Establishment and Constitution) Act, 1961, which followed doubts raised in *The State (Killian)* v. *Minister for Justice* [1954] I.R. 207, the whole court system depended on Article 58 which was not to be found in the published versions of the Constitution.

Although the legal system prescribed in Bunreacht na hÉireann is very similar to what already existed, one important addition, to which reference has already been made, should be noticed. The concept of the President acting as a check on the government on behalf of the people involves him being endowed with a number of discretionary powers. Among these is the power to refer a bill to the Supreme Court for an opinion as to whether the bill or any of its provisions is repugnant to the Constitution. It was the exercise of this power by President Ó Dálaigh in September 1976 that caused the clash with the Cosgrave Government and led to Ó Dálaigh's resignation and to an important judgement of the Supreme Court reserving its right to review resolutions of the Oireachtas declaring a state of emergency.[4]

Although, in forty years there were only five references under this provision, the Ó Dálaigh episode and the fact that in one case (*In re Article 26 of the Constitution and the School Attendance Bill, 1942,* [1943] I.R. 334) parts of the proposed legislation were in fact declared repugnant, show that this is an important safeguard which really works. It is the more important because four of these references concerned questions of personal rights of the citizen and the other, the reference of the Electoral Amendment Bill, 1961, concerned political rights.

While it is quite clearly not the case that the rights a citizen actually enjoys depend upon their being written down in a constitution or other document, it seems that in most countries people prefer that at least the most important rights and duties should be formally enunciated. The two earlier Irish Constitutions followed the majority view in this matter and, breaking with British tradition, included declarations of citizens' rights together with positive duties laid upon the state. Whereas the *Democratic Programme* of Dáil Éireann (1919) had a marked socialist tone, the declarations of the 1922 Constitution were liberal-democratic and traditional in character and were mostly couched in the form of restrictions on the government and Oireachtas, though they did include two positive principles (free elementary education and the public ownership of natural resources). Bunreacht na hÉireann introduces Roman

Catholic principles, combining them with the liberal-democratic rights of its predecessor in 'a much more elaborate series of guarantees'[5] laid out in five long Articles (nos. 40-44). In addition, it includes, in Article 45, what are are entitled 'Directive Principles of Social Policy' that also reflect the Catholic teaching of the time.

Most commentators on Bunreacht na hÉireann have remarked particularly on the Catholic influence it exhibits and characterize it as a Catholic constitution. According to Donal Barrington, it 'is in large part based on those principles which we associate in particular with the social teaching of the Catholic church, and the Papal encyclicals.'[6] In fact, it is in the rights articles, and Article 45 that this influence is chiefly to be seen. Elsewhere, the Constitution, though it is clearly Christian, is not specially Catholic, except in Articles 18 and 19, dealing with the composition of Seanad Éireann, where vocational representation is envisaged, and Article 15.3.1° which permits the establishment or recognition of 'functional or vocational councils'. (In fact, under none of these articles has vocationalism been achieved or, indeed, actively pursued.[7])

Vincent Grogan has pointed out that Articles 40-44 'follow closely in form and content a synthesis of Catholic social principles known as the Social Code, prepared by the International Union of Social Studies, Malines, Belgium.'[8] The work of this body, published in 1929, was publicly acknowledged by Pope Pius XI in his Encyclical *Quadragesimo Anno*. Their origins may, however, lie further back for in some places they reflect, as Brian Farrell has pointed out, 'strong echoes' of one of the discarded drafts of the Irish Free State Constitution prepared in the spring of 1922. This was the draft prepared by Professor Alfred O'Rahilly, and known as 'Draft C'.[9] O'Rahilly was, in Farrell's words, 'a vigorous and wide-ranging polemicist on social and political questions' who 'combined a passionate attachment to Catholic principles and values (as he saw them) with a special interest and relationship with Labour.' His 'Draft C', not published until 1970, 'seems to have had some influence on de Valera's thinking when he was preparing Bunreacht na hÉireann.'[10] Certainly, there is evidence that he consulted it between 1932 and 1934 when he was considering constitutional changes. In addition, he received advice, drafts and memoranda from a number of Catholic clergy, notably Father John Charles McQuaid C.S.Sp., later Archbishop of Dublin. He also read works by Dr. Michael Browne (later Bishop of Galway) and Dr. Cornelius Lucey (later Bishop of Cork). According to Lord Longford and T. P. O'Neill in their biography of de Valera, a work by Rev. A. Vermeersch S.J., *Code Sociale Esquisse d'une Synthèse Sociale Catholique* (Paris, 1934) was 'to prove of great help'.[11]

It is in these very same articles, however, that the liberal inheritance is most obvious and, following the pattern set in the Irish Free State Constitution, it is the liberal tradition that is in fact the most persistent influence running through Bunreacht na hÉireann as a whole. Explaining this, Barrington observes that the framers

> had to remember that they were not drawing up a 'Catholic Constitution for a Catholic People', but one for a people which in the past, had been torn by religious dissensions. They had to make a Constitution which would inspire the loyalty of an important Protestant minority, soon, they hoped, to be made larger by the solution of the partition problem.[12]

The result is a conflation of principles drawn from these two distinct traditions: 'certain of the fundamental rights are couched in language of a secular rationalist nature while others are clearly and strongly inspired by the Christian view of natural law.'[13] Although the mixture can be said on the whole to have served and satisfied the citizens of the Republic quite well, at least until recently, there was not a hope that it would 'inspire the loyalty of an important Protestant minority' in Northern Ireland. Yet for thirty years or more, few in the Republic were able and willing to recognize that fact.

The definition of the rights of the citizen in the Constitution and their classification and arrangement are in the view of the author of the only major work on the subject, John Kelly, 'somewhat unmethodical and in other ways unsatisfactory'.[14] They are grouped in five articles – Article 40, 'Personal Rights'; Article 41, 'The Family'; Article 42, 'Education'; Article 43, 'Private Property'; Article 44, 'Religion'. In addition, other articles elsewhere in the Constitution include important declarations of rights, notably Articles 15.5 and 39, and some sections of Articles 34-8.

Article 40, entitled 'Personal Rights', covers many of the personal and civil rights of the liberal tradition. It declares that all citizens shall be held equal before the law and that no citizen shall be deprived of liberty or have his home forcibly entered 'save in accordance with law', and it goes on to enunciate the right of habeas corpus. It guarantees 'subject to public order and morality' the rights of free expression 'including criticism of government policy', of peaceful assembly, and of forming associations and unions. It expressly forbids political, religious or class discrimination in legislation regulating these rights. In addition, there are provisions declaring that no titles of nobility shall be conferred by the state and that no title conferred by another state may be accepted by a citizen without the prior approval of the government. These reflect a rather austere and egalitarian republicanism. Article 15.5, which prevents the Oireachtas from declaring acts to be infringements of the law which were not so at the date of their commission, should also be noticed at this point, as should Article 39 that states clearly which are the only acts that can be considered as treason. Finally, it should be noted that Articles 34-8, which deal with the courts, contain declarations of important principles including the provision for public hearings 'save in such special and limited cases as may be prescribed by law', for the independence of the judges and their security of tenure and salary, and for limitations (though not very effective ones) on 'special courts'.

In general, Article 40 and the other provisions just mentioned reflect the same liberalism that inspired the enunciation of similar rights in the Irish Free State Constitution, tempered by qualifications on grounds of public order, morality and the maintenance of the authority of the state. On the other hand, they are widely enough drawn for the courts in recent years to infer rights that are not specifically stated. (See below, pp. 77-79)

The desirability of enunciating personal rights such as those in Article 40 is obvious. Equally obvious though, and accepted by most people, albeit sometimes reluctantly, is the need to provide the police and other authorities with discretionary powers that might erode and occasionally negate the enjoyment of rights apparently guaranteed by the Constitution or declared as essential or desirable in international declarations of human rights. Comparing the position in the Republic with that in the United States in 1971, Professor P. C. Bartholomew found that the Irish Constitution in many respects did not offer the protection afforded by the American Constitution. He thought that the limitations placed on the authorities by the courts 'are very definitely more casually regarded than are similar provisions in the Constitution of the United States.'[15] In addition, the state enjoys wide discretionary powers. If the Minister for Posts and Telegraphs thinks it is necessary, mail may be opened and telephones tapped and, in practice, the Dáil and the courts did not until recently afford much protection or redress. Matters such as the treatment of aliens, passports, naturalization and citizenship are in Ireland, as often elsewhere, inadequately regulated by the Constitution; are in part subject to ministerial discretion; and are only gradually coming under effective court scrutiny. In these matters and others – for this is by no means an exhaustive catalogue – Ireland is perhaps not all that different from most democratic countries.

In addition, the Irish government, like the governments of other countries, has to have power to act in 'emergencies' and to protect the 'security' of the state against 'subversion'. In such circumstances, arrangements intended to operate in normal, peaceful conditions are unequal to the situation and, indeed, may inhibit adequate preventive measures being taken. Michael O'Boyle put it thus:

> In legal theory the Government faces a difficult dilemma – on the one hand it is under an obligation to protect human rights, yet on the other hand it is under an obligation to protect the integrity of the state. In an emergency situation . . . these obligations conflict with each other. The effort to protect the state and its citizens will necessarily involve derogation from civil liberties. The dilemma is made more poignant by the very substantial risks that are inherent in such a situation.[16]

In Ireland, the legacies of the war of independence and the civil war in the shape of the intractable Northern Ireland problem and an ever-present I.R.A., have caused this dilemma to be almost continuously a live political issue. The passage of over half a century has not altered the situation.

Because of the threat or supposed threat of subversion or terrorism, all Irish governments have sought and obtained, or retained, considerable discretionary powers which, if exercised, could affect the personal liberties of the individual. A wide collection of such powers is vested in, or available to, ministers and their servants under the Offences against the State Act, 1940. These Acts restrict the publication or possession of 'treasonable', 'seditious' or 'incriminating' documents, and the holding of meetings or formation of associations for the purpose of forwarding the overthrow of the state. In using these powers, ministers and other officials have considerable discretion. Simply by issuing a proclamation declaring the need for them, the government acquires under these Acts powers to arrest without warrant, to detain without trial and to try in 'special courts' not necessarily composed of lawyers or using ordinary judicial procedures.

Thus the state has available a battery of powers that might appear surprising in their range in the light of Article 40. However, the drafters of that article (as indeed of the other rights articles) faced a problem that is well-nigh insoluble. In the words of K. C. Wheare, 'if a government is to be effective, few rights of its citizens can be stated in absolute form.' Hence, it is important to notice that Article 40 and the other rights articles are diluted with qualifications such as 'save in accordance with law', 'subject to public order and morality', and 'in the public interest', that can make them, as Wheare says, 'an empty promise'.[17] This was certainly the case in 1940 (*In re Article 26 and the Offences Against the State (Amendment) Bill, 1940* [1940] I.R. 470) when the Supreme Court decided that the words 'in accordance with law' meant in accordance with the law, whatever it is, as it exists at the time, and also that the detention of persons under the 1940 Act was 'not in the nature of a punishment' but 'a precautionary measure'. Although this extreme view was not subsequently upheld by the Court, the Government had, and still has, considerable elbow room.

Even so, more apparently is needed; and not only in Ireland, for as Michael O'Boyle has observed, most constitutions contain an emergency dispensing clause 'which enables the state to relax the customary constitutional restrictions and pass legislation which cannot be questioned by the courts.'[18] In addition, international declarations or conventions of human rights recognize the need for a state to have the right to 'derogate' in emergency. In the case of Ireland, Article 28.3.3° of Bunreacht na hÉireann gives such powers to the Oireachtas. Under the provisions of this Article, which was amended in 1939 and again in 1941, the Oireachtas may pass any law, however repugnant to the Constitution, 'which is expressed to be for the purpose of securing the public safety and the preservation of the state in time of war or armed rebellion'. The term 'time of war and armed rebellion' was defined and expanded at some length by the first and second amendments of the Constitution, so that the Article now reads as follows:

> 'time of war' includes a time when there is taking place an armed conflict in which the State is not a participant but in respect of which each of the Houses of the Oireachtas shall have resolved that, arising out of such armed conflict, a national emergency exists affecting the vital interests of the State and 'time of war or armed rebellion' includes such time after the termination of any war, or of any such armed conflict as aforesaid, or of an armed rebellion, as may elapse until each of the Houses of the Oireachtas shall have resolved that the national emergency occasioned by such war, armed conflict, or armed rebellion has ceased to exist.

Under the provisions of this article, both Houses of the Oireachtas on 2 September 1939 resolved (reasonably enough given the situation in western Europe) that, 'arising out of the armed conflict now taking place in Europe, a national emergency exists affecting the vital interests of the state.' Emergency Powers Acts covered by this declaration followed and were in force until 1946. The resolutions of September 1939 were not, however, rescinded at that time and the country thus remained in a state of 'national emergency' which continued until September 1976. Then, doubts having arisen whether the formula used in the 1939 resolution would cover proposed powers of detention in a new Emergency Powers Bill then deemed necessary because of the overspill effect of the civil war in Northern Ireland, the Oireachtas declared the 1939 emergency ended and resolved that another existed.

Thus, governments and the Oireachtas having for thirty-seven years retained in their hands, as Rory O'Hanlon put it, 'a power of the most far-reaching kind at a time when no one could argue that it was intended they should have it under the provisions of the Constitution',[19] it turned out not to be suitable when it was needed and had to be replaced. Whether the reservations of the Supreme Court expressed subsequently in *In re Article 26 of the Constitution and the Emergency Powers Bill, 1976* ([1977] I.R. 159, Irish Times, 16 October 1976) have interposed some measure of judicial safeguard after all is as yet uncertain. Although the Court found that bill not to be repugnant to the Constitution, it deliberately refuted the claim of the Attorney General that once the resolutions referred to in Article 28.3.3° have been passed, the Court has no jurisdiction to review their contents. 'The Court expressly reserves for future consideration the question whether the courts have jurisdiction to review such resolutions.'[20] It is thus now not at all clear that the question of what is 'a time of war or armed rebellion' is entirely a matter for the Oireachtas, in practice the government.

Clearly, Michael O'Boyle was right when he commented that the danger with powers of this type is that governments and their servants get used to having them. 'Succeeding generations of administrators inherit these powers as being efficient and correct and there develops over time an insensitivity to the human rights issues involved in an emergency situation.' In such circumstances there might occur 'a gradual erosion of concern for civil liberties' which could bring in its train 'a mounting lack of confidence in institutions of the state and a solid disrespect for the police and the army.'[21] The recent history of Northern Ireland demonstrates clearly the onset and course of what might be called the emergency powers syndrome. However, the attitudes of the courts in the Republic, particularly of the Supreme Court and the Special Criminal Court recently, have done something to slow up this all-too-easy regression. An adequate procedure for examining complaints against the Gardaí could do more, but successive governments have resisted any proposal for independent inquiry. To suggest it has sometimes been taken as attempting to hinder security operations and as unwarranted criticism of 'a fine body of men'. Unhappily, by 1977, there were some signs that the Republic was beginning to move inexorably down the same dangerous slope as Northern Ireland.

The clearest and most unequivocal enunciation of Catholic principles in Bunreacht na hÉireann is to be found in Articles 41 and 42 which deal with the family and education. Kelly considered them 'wholly inspired by Christian (or, more specifically, by Catholic) orthodoxy, in particular by well-known encyclicals of modern Popes', and he mentions two in particular, both of Pius XI, namely *Divini Illius Magistri* (English title – On the Christian Education of Youth, 1929) and *Casti Connubii* (English title – On Christian Marriage, 1930). It is these Articles 'above everything else in the Constitution, which have excited most admiration among Catholic observers', and they are 'the only feature of the Fundamental Rights declarations which is original and unusual'.[22]

In Article 41 it is declared that 'the State recognises the Family as the natural primary and fundamental unit group of society, and as a moral institution possessing inalienable and imprescriptible rights, antecedent and superior to all positive laws.' Naturally, therefore, the state guarantees to protect the family. It is pledged to guard the institution of marriage, and the enactment of laws granting a dissolution of marriage is forbidden. Going further, the Constitution 'also forbids a person who has been divorced abroad and whose marriage is "a subsisting valid marriage" under Irish law, to remarry within the Republic while the original spouse is alive.'[23] Even persons whose marriages have been 'annulled' by the Catholic Church, a procedure that has been made easier in recent years, may not legally remarry in Ireland. In addition, the Constitution recognizes the special position of mothers and it declares that 'the State shall, therefore, endeavour to ensure that mothers shall not be obliged by economic necessity to engage in labour to the neglect of their duties in the home.'

The primacy of the family is further underpinned in Article 42 which deals with education. The family is recognized as 'the primary and natural educator' of the child. Parents are declared to have 'the inalienable right and duty' to provide for the education of their children and they are free to provide it in their homes or in any schools, private or state, that they wish. However, the state 'as guardian of the common good' shall require the children to receive 'a certain minimum education', and it may in exceptional cases 'supply the place of the parents' where these have failed. The State is to provide free primary education and, because secondary education is largely in the hands of private, mostly religious, organizations, the article provides that the State is to 'endeavour to supplement and give reasonable aid to private and corporate educational initiative, and, when the public good requires it, provide other educational facilities . . .'

Catholic principles are evident also in Article 43 where the right to private property is stated with important qualifications. Both in its tone and content it is 'intended . . . to reproduce Catholic teaching on the matter.'[24] This is of course far from the nineteenth century liberal position: indeed it might seem to permit of moderately socialist and redistributive policies, particularly since the encyclical *Mater et Magistra* (1961) of Pope John XXIII. However, Catholic limitations on private property and the rights of private owners derive from assumptions very different from those of socialism, as the wording of the Constitution makes clear. The state 'acknowledges that man, in virtue of his rational being, has the natural right, antecedent to positive law, to the private ownership of external goods.' Accordingly, the State 'guarantees to pass no law attempting to abolish' it. However, the exercise of property rights 'ought, in civil society, to be regulated by the principles of social justice' and, hence, the State 'may as occasion requires delimit by law the exercise of the said rights with a view to reconciling their exercise with the exigencies of the common good.'

This is another notable example of the kind of qualification that is a feature of the fundamental rights Articles and to which attention has been drawn. Wheare has pointed to it as 'a classic example of giving a right with one hand and taking it back with the other.'[25] However, as John Kelly pointed out, this is inherent in the Catholic position on this issue, and he quoted Mgr. John Ryan's view that, according to Catholic teaching, 'where the line should be drawn between (sic) State ownership which encroaches upon the right of private property, cannot be exactly described beforehand. The question is entirely one of expediency and human welfare.'[26] In connection with property, we should also notice Article 10 which, repeating Article 11 of the Irish Free State Constitution, declares that the State owns all natural resources. This Article seems not to be wholly reconcilable with Article 43.

It was with Article 44, on religious liberty, that the major problem of reconciling different principles arose and it was with this article that de Valera had most trouble. Here, more than anywhere else, he had to take into account not only Catholic precepts on the treatment of religion by the state, but also the aspirations of the majority for a united Ireland, the recent history of independence and partition, the fears of the Protestants on both sides of the border and the guarantees on religion incorporated in the Irish Free State Constitution. Though he consulted a number of senior clergy including the Papal Nuncio, Cardinal MacRory and the heads of churches other than the Catholic church, the eventual draft was his own.[27] Not surprisingly this article has been the most contentious one in Bunreacht na hÉireann, at first coming under attack by Catholic zealots for not being Catholic enough and, later, for being too Catholic or too rigidly Catholic. It is one of the few articles to have been amended (see below, page 67).

In the form in which it existed for thirty-five years, it recognized 'the special position of the Holy Catholic Apostolic and Roman Church as the guardian of the Faith professed by the great majority of the citizens'; and it also recognized other religious denominations which existed in the community at the time of enactment. Further, it assured 'freedom of conscience and the free profession and practice of religion'. The state guaranteed not to endow any religion; not to impose any disabilities on religious grounds; not to discriminate in providing aid for schools; and not to interfere with church property compulsorily save for 'necessary works of public utility and on payment of compensation.'

De Valera's solution to a difficult problem was less than satisfactory according to the Catholic teaching of the time as some understood it. Following the precepts embodied in the Encyclical *Immortale Dei* (1885) of Pope Leo XIII and elsewhere, the view was widely held in Ireland that it was the duty of rulers to make a public profession of religion and to support it – 'not such religion as they may have a preference for, but the religion which God enjoins, and which certain and most clear marks show to be the only one true religion.'[27]

On the other hand, the compromise – for most saw it as such – commended itself to more enlightened Catholic commentators. In Donal Barrington's words, 'it must be freely admitted that the position of the Church under the Irish Constitution falls short of the ideal',[29] but he contended that the reasons for the position taken up were justified under the circumstances and that the situation, if not ideal, was satisfactory according to Catholic principles themselves. He added: 'the toleration shown by Article 44 has . . . nothing in common with the religious indifferentism so often condemned by the Popes, but is an expression of one of the noblest Christian virtues.'[30] The Rev. Dr Enda McDonagh came to much the same conclusion. Although he did not agree with Barrington that there could in principle be a universally ideal solution of church-state relations and argued that 'no particular form of institutionalizing harmony between Church and State is demanded by Catholic doctrine', he concluded that the Irish Constitution 'is not an ideal solution . . . but is a sound application of the general principles of Catholic teaching to the Irish circumstances of the day.'[31]

The unmistakable sound of liberal-minded Catholics in agony revealed in these quotations may seem strange today. Decisions taken at the Second Vatican Council made it clear that the Catholic Church no longer sought any special recognition or privileged position. In the late sixties, Article 44 came under criticism from the other direction, criticism that became the sharper with the outbreak of civil war in Northern Ireland. In 1972, the clauses recognizing 'the special position' of the Catholic Church and according recognition to named religions were deleted by the fifth amendment to the Constitution.[32]

Constitutions are not addressed to lawyers alone, but are for the people as a whole and in particular their public representatives. This was clearly recognized in the Irish case, for it is to legislators explicitly that Article 45, entitled 'Directive Principles of Social Policy', is addressed. Indeed, the courts seem to be excluded: 'The principles of policy set forth in this Article are intended for the general guidance of the Oireachtas' and 'shall not be cognisable by any court'.[33] This is a rather unusual type of provision to find in a Constitution, but it occurred in the Spanish Republican Constitution of 1931, and, following the Irish example, it was used by India, Pakistan and Burma.[34]

The principles laid down in Article 45 to a certain extent supplement the fundamental rights articles, adding as they do a set of 'welfare state' aims. In this respect they recall the *Democratic Programme* of 1919, but, whereas that document showed signs of socialist influence, Article 45, like the rights articles, is largely based on Catholic teaching and couched in Catholic terms. The state is to promote the welfare of all 'by securing and protecting as effectively as it may a social order in which justice and charity shall inform all the institutions of the national life.' It is to seek to ensure that all, men and women, 'may through their occupations find the means of making reasonable provision for their domestic needs.' It should have a special care for the weaker in the community and should ensure that people, especially women and children, should not be forced to take up jobs 'unsuited to their sex, age or strength'.

The Catholic position is also evident in the sections of Article 45 on property and business enterprise. The State should seek to arrange that ownership and control of resources be so distributed amongst persons and classes 'as best to subserve the common good.' Competition should not be allowed to result in a concentration of ownership of commodities in the hands of a few 'to the common detriment'; the state should seek to ensure that private enterprise be conducted efficiently; and the public should be protected against 'unjust' exploitation. In addition, 'the state shall favour and, where necessary, supplement private initiative in industry and commerce', and credit should be controlled in the interests of the community. Finally, we should notice the declaration of a social aim reflecting the ideal of a rural, peasant-owner society that was so dear to the heart of de Valera, for the state is directed to attempt to secure 'that there may be established on the land in economic security as many families as . . . practicable.'

Has the inclusion of these principles influenced the pattern of Irish social development as was intended? It is difficult to give an answer. The policy of land division was already well established. On the other hand, Ireland is not notably more concerned about the weak in the community than other western countries; in some respects social services are poor, even taking into account the relative poverty of the country. Also, one seldom hears references made to this Article either in the Oireachtas or outside, and only one of its sections seems to have become a much quoted and effective working principle – that which enjoins the state to favour and, where necessary, supplement, private initiative.

Despite the apparent finality of the wording used in Article 45, the courts have not been completely excluded from considering its provisions. On the contrary, as Professor R. F. V. Heuston has pointed out, in recent years 'an amazingly wide interpretation has been given to Article 45'. In giving judgements in a number of cases from the early seventies onwards, the courts have held that the Directive Principles may be considered in some circumstances. Notably, it has been held, in Heuston's words, 'that a court may consider these principles when considering whether the constitutional right claimed by a citizen exists.'[35]

One might ask why in the first place an attempt was made to inhibit the courts from interpreting and applying the principles contained in Article 45, while others elsewhere in the Constitution are wholly within their ambit except in times of emergency. To begin with, it has to be remembered that in the thirties economic and social matters of the kind dealt with in Article 45 were not justiciable rights or even recognized rights in many liberal democratic states such as those of the British Commonwealth. More particularly, de Valera, populist leader as he then still was, had a considerable suspicion of the judges of that time, trained as they were in the British tradition and appointed in the case of most of them by Cumann na nGaedheal governments. He believed that it was to the Oireachtas that one should look for the securing and developing of citizens' rights. He saw Articles 40-44 as well as Article 45 as 'headlines with regard to the things that the legislature should aim at.'[36] He did not think that it was desirable to have the courts thwart the Oireachtas, for he believed that 'the legislature has the responsibility of working in the public interest and of seeing, in the passing of its laws, that the rights of the individual, as an individual, and the rights of the community, as a community, do not conflict and are properly coordinated. That is the duty of the legislature.'[37]

It is clear from this statement and others like it that de Valera took a very narrow view of the functions and role of the courts. Looking back on the forty year's experience of judicial review, it is, however, obvious that the opportunities the courts have to interpret the Constitution and their potential influence in developing it are considerable. We return to this important matter in Chapter 8 below.

PART THREE
Constitutional Development

Chapter 7

AMENDMENT

Irish constitutions were a product of the inter-war period, the 'Indian summer of constitutional democracy', as Karl Loewenstein called it.'[1] In Ireland's case, that summer was long drawn out for until recently neither war nor revolution afflicted the island to generate social and political strains of the kind that were experienced in some other western European countries after 1939. True, the Irish Free State Constitution was much amended, but that was because, in the eyes of de Valera and the majority in the Twenty-six counties, it never did effect the desired constitutional arrangements and was thus faulty, and, for some, of doubtful validity. These matters settled to de Valera's satisfaction – and the country's – Ireland like the stable western countries of the time possessed, in Loewenstein's terminology, a 'normative' constitution:

> Once a constitutional order has been formally accepted by a nation, it is not only valid in the sense of being legal but also real in the sense of being fully activated and effective. If this is the case, a constitution is normative.[2]

In these circumstances, Bunreacht na hÉireann came to be viewed, to borrow Bagehot's phrase, as 'a grand and achieved result', the more so since its author dominated the country's politics for most of the next quarter of a century. The Irish judiciary, a potential source of change, was conservative in interpreting his handiwork for even longer. Consequently, there was little or no development of the Constitution until recently.

Inevitably, of course, the efflux of time brought incongruencies between some of the rules enshrined in the Constitution, no matter how flexibly these were interpreted, and reality or the changing values of the community. In Ireland's case, social and political changes eventually came with a rush that seemed the greater because of the stability, even stagnation, of the forties and fifties. The engines of change were the movement in Catholic thought and practice following the Second Vatican Council (1962-5) that came to be called *aggiornamento,* the civil war in Northern Ireland from 1969, and Ireland's accession to the European Communities (1972). Thus the constitutional history of Ireland since 1937 consists of more than a quarter of a century of stasis followed, on the one hand, by a burst of judicial creativity in interpreting the Constitution, and, on the other, by the first instalment of what will eventually be a radical revision by way of amendment or replacement.

In this chapter, we shall examine the processes and history of constitutional amendment and in Chapter 8, judicial interpretation. These chapters will be followed by a survey of the impact of the forces for change, namely, first, Ireland's accession to the European Communities and, second, the effect of events in Northern Ireland which have raised questions about the suitability of Bunreacht na hÉireann for a thirty-two county, two community republic and have become enmeshed with the debate about liberalisation and secularisation of the Constitution induced by *aggiornamento.*

It would be unrealistic to expect a constitution, however carefully prepared and widely accepted, not to need changing. To begin with, there are likely to be problems of transition from one constitution to the next that will either require temporary arrangements or subsequent changes in the constitution. Next, it is obviously prudent to envisage a 'running in' period. There will inevitably be need to clarify points found by early experience to be obscure, or to be inadequately covered or infelicitously phrased; to remedy errors; and, where more than one language is involved, to iron out discordances. Finally, permanent arrangements for change need to be spelled out in the constitution itself. All of these provisions for change were provided for in Bunreacht na hÉireann as it was 'enacted' i.e. approved by the people in July 1937. Only the last, the normal provisions for amending the Constitution, now remain embodied in the official text; but it is important to realise that the others were originally there and that by means of them important matters were disposed of and significant changes made.

'Transitory Provisions' were embodied in Articles 51-63 of the Constitution, and are no longer in the official text.[3] These included a provision for amending the Constitution itself for a limited period on the authority of the Oireachtas alone; for the election of the first Seanad under the new arrangements; for deeming the authorities of the state under the Irish Free State Constitution – the Dáil and its officers, the government, the courts and the judges, the Attorney General, the Comptroller and Auditor General, and the defence and police forces – to be the appropriate authorities under Bunreacht na hÉireann; for the entry into office of the President and, pending that event, for a presidential commission; for the coming into force of Bunreacht na hÉireann; and for the deposit of an official copy of the text of the Constitution in the office of the Registrar of the Supreme Court.

In addition, provision was made in the Transitory Provisions – in Articles 52 and 53 – for the provisions themselves to be 'omitted from every official text of the Constitution' after certain specified dates: in the case of Article 51, the temporary amending procedure, after three years; in the case of all the other articles, 'after the date on which the President shall have entered upon his office' i.e. June, 1938. Nevertheless, Articles 52-63 were, 'notwithstanding such omission to continue to have the force of law'. Although this provision subsequently gave rise to some heavy humour from opposition deputies when Articles that were absent from published copies were referred to in the Dáil and even amended, the continued existence in force of one at least, Article 58, came in very handy to provide a legal underpinning for the courts as late as 1954 when their legality was challenged.[4]

Although Bunreacht na hÉireann was eventually to be a 'rigid' constitution i.e. to amend it requires special procedures involving more than the ordinary legislative process, one of the Transitory Provisions, Article 51, provided that any part of the Constitution could be amended by the Oireachtas within a period of three years after the date on which the first President 'shall have entered upon his office', which was June, 1938. Thus, until June 1941 constitutional amendment was a matter for the Oireachtas, except when a proposal was in the opinion of the President 'of such a character and importance that the will of the people thereon ought to be ascertained by referendum.' Two amendment acts were passed under Article 51; the first, a crisis measure in September 1939; the second, a collection of changes lumped together and collectively referred to as the Second Amendment of the Constitution Act, 1941.

The First Amendment of the Constitution Act, 1939, was occasioned by the outbreak of the war in Europe.[5] Article 28.3.3°, the article which in emergency gives the Oireachtas the power to enact legislation however repugnant to the Constitution, in its original form confined that power to 'time of war or armed rebellion'. In introducing the amendment to a hastily recalled Dáil on a Saturday afternoon (2 September 1939), de Valera recalled the already declared aim of the Government, viz. 'in case of a European war, to keep this country, if at all possible, out of it.' Emergency measures were going to be needed, but 'some doubt was expressed by legal officers as to whether "time of war" might not be narrowly interpreted by courts to mean a time in which the state was actually a participant, a belligerent.'[6] This had not occurred to people when the Constitution was being prepared and considered.

The First Amendment Act defined and extended the meaning of 'time of war' by adding the following words:

> In this sub-section 'time of war' includes a time when there is taking place an armed conflict in which the state is not a participant but in respect of which each of the Houses of the Oireachtas shall have resolved that, arising out of such armed conflict, a national emergency exists affecting the vital interests of the state.

The resolution needed to give the Oireachtas its extended powers followed post-haste and the first bill under these provisions, the Emergency Powers Bill, 1939, was as swiftly enacted. By 2.30 a.m. the next morning, the Dáil, its own programme dealt with, was sitting around waiting for the Seanad to complete the same programme.

With a speed that the circumstances, all agreed, seemed to demand, Ireland was put on an emergency footing. Rightly, as it turned out, William Norton, the Labour Party leader, and others sought assurances that the constitutional amendment would not be abused. 'If Britain is at war, a state of national emergency must exist here',[7] Norton conceded, but he wished to be assured that a state of emergency would not be occasioned by, or justified on foot of, far away wars as for example, he instanced, between China and Japan. 'Certainly, as far as the government is concerned we give that assurance' was de Valera's reply.[8] Nevertheless, the first – admittedly justified – step had been taken on a road that could make a mockery of constitutional guarantees and rights. The next step, equally justified it seemed – for do they not all seem to be so at the time? – was taken in the Second Amendment of the Constitution Act, 1941, less than two years later.

The Second Amendment Act was occasioned by the coming to an end of the three-year period during which constitutional amendments required only Oireachtas approval. A systematic appraisal was undertaken by the central departments and suggestions were made to the Government. Those approved – a miscellaneous selection – were incorporated in a single bill. Most were not of importance, consisting as they did of minor additions, clarifications, and changes in the Irish text occasioned by inaccurate translation or editing errors in the original. More important were alterations in Articles 26 and 34, which had the effect of prohibiting the Supreme Court, when giving a judgement, from pronouncing or disclosing the existence of any opinion other than that of the majority, in Article 40 (on *habeas corpus*) and in Article 56 (on the rights of transferred officers), an Article that had by that time disappeared from the official text. Though of some significance, they were, in the Government's view, only intended to clarify the existing position rather than to introduce something which was 'fundamentally new'.[9]

Undoubtedly the most important amendment was another addition to Article 28.3.3° which has had far-reaching consequences. It permitted an emergency occasioned by a time of war or armed rebellion to be extended beyond the cessation of actual hostilities:

> ... time of war or armed rebellion includes such time after the termination of any war, or of any such armed conflict as aforesaid or of an armed rebellion, as may elapse until each of the Houses of the Oireachtas shall have resolved that the national emergency occasioned by such war, armed conflict, or armed rebellion has ceased to exist.

It might well be difficult, de Valera explained, to say exactly when a war ends and, in any case, after a war 'you do not quite get back to a position of peace.'[10] In opposing the amendment, an opposition front bench speaker, Professor John Marcus O'Sullivan, was prescient when he said 'surely the powers which this House unhesitatingly gave the Government to deal with internal trouble in 1939 were sufficiently wide without making almost permanent this formal wiping away of what is left of constitutional guarantees for personal liberty.'[11]

Under the power given by this amendment, the state of national emergency created by the resolution of September 1939 was kept in being until September 1976; and then – such are the powers of the Oireachtas under Article 28.3.3° in its final form – it was immediately resolved that another state of emergency existed.[12] Throughout these years a state of emergency could – of course – be justified by those in office: '... experience has shown how difficult it was to deal with an emergency with the means available under a rigid constitution', Patrick McGilligan, a lawyer and a former minister then in opposition, told a meeting in 1958. Two years later, Seán Lemass, then Taoiseach, informed the Dáil that he did not consider it would be 'an appropriate time' to rescind the resolution, 'having regard', as he put it, 'to the present very unsettled international situation.' In 1964, it was still 'the international situation' plus 'the speed of delivery of the weapons now available' which caused his Government 'to consider it unwise to move the terminating resolutions.'[13] Clearly, powers acquired in and for an emergency soon came to be regarded as permanently essential by the governments, no matter of what party, that had them.

The tidying-up period over, de Valera was evidently satisfied with his handiwork. From 1941 until 1972, Bunreacht na hÉireann remained unchanged. Once the transitional arrangements for amendment were superseded, Ireland's Constitution was both in form and in fact a 'rigid' constitution.

The procedures for amendment are covered in Articles 46 and 47 and in legislation – principally the Referendum Act 1942 (No. 8), the Electoral Act, 1963 (No. 19), and the Electoral (Amendment) Act 1972 (No. 4). Article 46 provides that a proposal for amendment must be initiated in Dáil Éireann and, having been passed or deemed to have been passed by both houses, must be 'submitted by referendum to the decision of the people . . .' For a proposal to be held to have been approved by the people, it must, under Article 47, have the support of a majority of those voting. The franchise is the same as that for Dáil elections. A bill to amend the Constitution cannot contain any other proposal, but a referendum on such a bill can be held on the same day as a general election or a presidential election.[14]

Originally, i.e. under the Referendum Act, 1942, the rules covering the form of the ballot paper prescribed that the proposal must 'be stated on the ballot paper in the same terms as nearly as may be as such proposal is stated in the Bill.' The obvious problems that this might cause arose on the very first occasion on which the provisions were to be used. In 1959, when the Government was about to submit to the people a 'bill running to several pages', it had hurriedly to introduce and get enacted the Referendum (Amendment) Act, 1959, which provided that a proposal that is the subject of a referendum would be stated on the ballot paper by citing the bill in which it is contained by its 'short title.'[15] The question now asked on the ballot paper is:

> Do you approve of the proposal to amend the Constitution contained in the undermentioned Bill?
>
> N[th] AMENDMENT OF THE CONSTITUTION BILL [date]

In arguing for this form, the Minister for Local Government of the day pointed out that it would be both 'quite impracticable' to print a long bill on the ballot paper and 'unreasonable to expect a voter to read a long document of that kind.'[16] For those interested, copies of the bill to be voted on are placed in post offices and may be inspected; and, more important, it is the practice to describe the purpose and effect of the proposal on the polling card, a card which is sent by post to each registered elector prior to polling day. Such explanations have varied from the twenty-eight words that were required to describe the Fourth Amendment Bill (to lower the voting age) to a few hundred, as in the case of the Third Amendment Bill, 1971 (accession to the E.E.C.) which recited the text of the proposed addition and explained in a sentence what the purpose of the addition was; and the Fifth Amendment Bill (to alter Article 44), which laid out in full both what was to be deleted and how the article would then read. Perhaps this solution of an admittedly difficult problem is as practicable as any.

Up to the end of 1977, only three amendments had been made under this procedure–all of them in 1972–and two proposals passed the Oireachtas had been rejected. Thus, the experience with Bunreacht na hÉireann has been in sharp contrast to that with the Irish Free State Constitution which was amended twenty-seven times between 1922 and 1937. Until the late sixties at least, the general verdict was, as John Kelly then observed, that 'by and large it has given satisfaction'. Although by that time a Dáil committee to advise on the revision of the Constitution had reported, Kelly gave it as his opinion that 'scarcely a single one of the topics dealt with by the Committee represents an issue on which change has been demanded by even a section of the public.'[17] In fact, during the thirty years from 1937 to 1967 only two matters were raised in any significant way – the position of the Catholic Church vis-à-vis the state and the voting system.

The section of Article 44 that referred to the special position of the Catholic Church was, as we have seen, a compromise of de Valera's own making, and it was far from acceptable to a small minority of zealous Catholics. During the forties, a tiny but active Catholic organization called *Maria Duce,* led by Father Denis Fahey, campaigned vigorously for its amendment and for a while attracted some support, some of its meetings being attended by crowds numbered in thousands. In a memorandum addressed to the Hierarchy, public bodies and members of the Oireachtas, the organization complained that, as it stood, Article 44 'merely recognizes the Catholic Church as the church of the majority of

Irishmen, not as the one true church founded by our Divine Lord.' In 1949, *Maria Duce* organized a petition urging an amendment of the Constitution.[18] Although it had the support of a few clergy and perhaps even an individual politician or two, the agitation came to nothing without the backing of either a political party or the Hierarchy. Twenty years later, there were to be more complaints about Article 44, but this time on the grounds not that it did not go far enough, but that it went altogether too far (see below p. 68).

More serious, because they were backed by the government of the day, were the attempts to alter the voting system; and more remarkable too, because, despite government backing, they were defeated. That system, 'proportional representation by means of the single transferable vote', as the Constitution describes it, was the system both favoured by Arthur Griffith and Sinn Féin, and sought by the British in the negotiations leading up to the Treaty as a safeguard for the Southern Unionists, and it was accordingly prescribed in the Irish Free State Constitution. When, in the middle thirties, de Valera was preparing Bunreacht na hÉireann, it was perhaps too soon after the events and circumstances that had dictated its inclusion in the first place to seek to replace it; but, in any case, it had worked well and there is little evidence that anyone was then seeking a change. In fact, it was not until the late fifties, when he was coming to the end of his last long period in office that de Valera raised the issue.

The Third Amendment of the Constitution Bill, 1958, provided for the replacement of the 40 multi-seat constituencies by 100-150 single-seat constituencies and the substitution of the single non-transferable vote (the so-called straight vote) for the single transferable vote, the candidate obtaining the most votes in each constituency to win the seat. The arguments advanced for altering the existing system centred on the unsatisfactory effects of retaining P.R. (as the system is usually known in Ireland) in the changed political situation following the resolution of most of the outstanding constitutional issues and the softening of attitudes in respect of those that still remained. De Valera himself put it thus:

> P.R. has not, in my opinion, in recent times worked out well ... it worked very well for a time because there were issues so large in the public eye that they dominated all other issues, and, therefore, the people voted on one side or the other. Some of this stability was acquired rather in spite of the system ... The whole effect of the present system of P.R. has been to cause a multiplicity of parties ... Under the system of straight voting they will have to unite beforehand not after.[19]

Evidently also, de Valera intended that the change was to be his legacy to Fianna Fáil as he relinquished the leadership. Since he was to be a candidate at the Presidential election held on the same day as the referendum, and would surely be elected, his prestige, it was thought, would ensure the passage of the amendment. But it did not; in a poll of 58 per cent, the proposal was narrowly defeated – 453,322 votes (48.2 per cent) for; 486,989 votes (51.8 per cent) against. The importance and value of the constitutional amendment procedure as a democratic device were amply demonstrated on this its first trial, a demonstration that was to be repeated nine years later.

On this occasion, the Third Amendment of the Constitution Bill, 1968, which proposed wider limits of tolerance in constituency populations – a much needed change caused by a restrictive High Court judgement (*O'Donovan* v. *Attorney General* [1961] I.R. 114) – and the Fourth Amendment of the Constitution Bill, 1968, which sought to substitute the 'straight vote' system for P.R., to establish a constituency boundary commission and to provide for the automatic return of the Ceann Comhairle, were more decisively rejected by the electorate. Not only did the opposition parties oppose the bill arguing that, given the pattern of party support in the country, this was a naked bid for power for a generation to come, but the trade union movement also campaigned vigorously against it. On the other side, some of the Fianna Fáil Deputies themselves evidently did not welcome a change in the election system and campaigned, if at all, only casually. The results (in a turn-out of 66 per cent), a defeat by 656,803 (60.8 per cent) to 424,185 (39.2 per cent) on the issue of the tolerance in constituency populations and by 657,898 (60.8 per cent) to 423,496 (39.2 per cent) on the proposal to abolish P.R., suggested strongly that some Fianna Fáil supporters voted against their party's proposals. Journalists and others at the time commented on a credibility gap between the party leaders and some of their supporters. It is unlikely that politicians of any party will put the matter to the test again for a long while.

It is arguable that Fianna Fáil's importunity in persisting with its attempt to change the election system might have inhibited other changes that were perhaps more widely acceptable, at least among politicians. For, by this time, deliberate processes for initiating change had been instituted. Characteristically, it was Seán Lemass who triggered them off. As part of his efforts to modernize Irish politics that extended to initiating new policies, e.g. towards Northern Ireland, and to setting up a body to review the public service, he proposed a review of the Constitution. Although he recognized that the principles of the Constitution continued to have a strong appeal, he argued that 'the manner in which these principles were expressed and the procedures by which it was decided to apply them might not, however, be as suitable to our present requirements as they were thirty years ago.' In any case, the Supreme Court had in some instances interpreted the Constitution 'in a way its drafters had not expected or intended.' He thought there was 'a case for carrying out a general review of the provisions of the Constitution.'[20] Repeating his proposal in the Dáil a week later, he made it clear that he was thinking of it as a routine operation: such a review ought to be undertaken 'every twenty-five years or so.'[21]

In August 1966, the three political parties represented in the Dáil agreed that 'an informal committee' of Deputies and Senators should be set up 'to review the constitutional, legislative and institutional bases of government.' In its report published in December 1967, this committee acknowledged that in general Bunreacht na hÉireann continued to give satisfaction: 'we are not aware of any public demand for a change in the basic structure of the Constitution.'[22] However, it systematically reviewed the whole text and dealt with twenty-seven matters either by way of recommendation where the members were unanimous or, where they were not, by expounding the arguments for and against changes, 'leaving it to the government of the day to decide the items which should be selected for inclusion in any legislative proposals that may emerge.'[23]

This, intended as an 'interim' report, was in fact the committee's only report because the Government chose to go forward on only one of the issues it dealt with, namely the election system. That was of course a highly contentious matter on which the committee had expressed no agreed recommendation. The all-party approach to constitutional change was thus shattered and, in spite of another attempt to work by way of such a committee, it has never been renewed. This then was a false start. However, in boldly raising a number of important issues such as the extent of the state (Article 3), divorce and the special position of the Catholic Church – on all of which, surprisingly, the members were agreed – the committee sparked off discussion and controversy. In the course of it, the pattern of public opinion became clear. Changing Article 3 and dealing with divorce carried great political risks, though their consideration in a Northern Ireland context from 1969 onwards complicated the picture; the section according a 'special position' to the Catholic Church was a different matter, being ripe for removal.

Before it was dealt with, however, a matter which in its timing was not wholly within the control of the Irish government arose: accession to the European Communities.

Ireland's negotiations to become a member of the European Communities came to a successful conclusion in January 1972 when a treaty of accession was signed. The implications of membership had been carefully investigated by the Government over a number of years.[24] Amongst these was the need to amend the Constitution. 'As it is at present,' John Temple Lang wrote, 'the Irish Constitution does not allow the legislature to confer on the Community institutions the powers which belong to them under the Treaties, so as to make these powers effective under Irish law.'[25] In a Government White Paper published in April 1970, mention was made of a number of articles which needed to be considered in this regard, but the Government's eventual solution, embodied in the Third Amendment of the Constitution Bill, 1971, was a simple change in Article 29.4, consisting of the addition of a third subsection as follows:

> 3° The State may become a member of the European Coal and Steel Community (established by Treaty signed at Paris on the 18th day of April, 1951), the European Economic Community (established by Treaty signed at Rome on the 25th day of March, 1957) and the European Atomic Energy Community (established by Treaty signed at Rome on the 25th day of March, 1957). No provision of this Constitution invalidates laws enacted, acts done or measures adopted by the State necessitated by the obligations of membership of the Communities or prevents laws enacted, acts done or measures adopted by the Communities, or institutions thereof, from having the force of law in the State.

This, it was held, would allow the state to honour its obligations while obviating the need to make a whole series of changes, some of which would present considerable difficulties.

The two largest parties, Fianna Fáil and Fine Gael, had long been in favour of Ireland joining the Communities and the outcome of the referendum was, therefore, virtually certain. Their spokesmen stressed the economic advantages, both long term (jobs, higher prices for Irish exports, and aid) and immediate (the transfer of farm subsidies from the Irish Exchequer to the E.E.C. budget); and they pointed out the disadvantages of attempting to pursue any other course of action now that the United Kingdom, Ireland's biggest customer and major supplier, was joining. They conceded that there would be price increases but these would be small. They argued that membership 'would enable both parts of Ireland to achieve, in the economic and social spheres, a unity and an equality which has long been aspired to.'[26]

The Labour Party, on the other hand, opposed entry and argued for the alternative of an association or trading agreement with the E.E.C.; Ireland was not developed enough 'to take the strains of full membership', Corish, its leader, argued: 'the Government's decision. . . had placed in jeopardy the jobs and standard of living of our people.'[27] Labour's forecasts on jobs and prices contrasted sharply with those of their opponents. Although bread and butter issues were without doubt the major themes of the campaign, a minor but persistent theme was that of sovereignty. A Labour Deputy, David Thornley, asserted that 'in the long run our national sovereignty could be completely eroded . . . the objective in the E.E.C., let us be clear, is one parliament and one government for Europe.'[28] On the contrary, Lynch argued, the proposed amendment did not cover any future political community: 'such a political community would have to be based on a new and separate treaty.'[29]

Labour was joined by the Irish Congress of Trade Unions which mounted its own campaign and by Sinn Féin and other republican and socialist republican movements. A considerable publicity campaign was mounted by *ad hoc* groups, notably the Common Market Defence Campaign and the Common Market Study Group: the latter in particular produced the most reasoned and thoughtful case against entry. However, the anti-marketeers complained with justification that they were at a hopeless disadvantage against the full resources of the state machine, joined during the campaign by major agricultural and industrial organizations both in the public and private sectors. In particular, farmers' organizations mounted 'the biggest and most intensive campaign ever undertaken.'[30]

The result of the Referendum held on 10 May 1972 was an overwhelming 'yes'. In a high poll (71 per cent), 1,041,890 (83 per cent) voted 'yes' and 211,891 (17 per cent) voted 'no'. Perhaps the intervention of militant republicans had frightened some people out of the 'no' camp and caused them to vote 'yes', but the big poll and the great size of the 'yes' vote was largely due to the combination of the two biggest parties and the zealous efforts of the farmers' organizations. Lynch called it 'a great moment in history'[31]: to tell the truth, it was a moment at which considerations of material gain, not least of higher farm prices, loomed larger than any loftier motives such as European unity.

Equally decisive were the votes in favour of the fourth and fifth amendments, both decided on the same day, 7 December 1972; not surprisingly, since both were supported by all parties in the Dáil. The fact that the two issues, votes at eighteen and the removal of the special position of the Catholic Church, were linked together in this way and in the preceding electoral campaign, such as it was, probably accounts for the similarity in the results. Only 51 per cent voted, for the outcomes were foregone conclusions and not much political effort was put into the campaign. The Fourth Amendment of the Constitution Bill – which lowered the minimum voting age prescribed in Article 16.1.2° from twenty-one to eighteen years – was passed by 724,836 votes (84.5 per cent) to 131,154: the Fifth Amendment of the Constitution Bill, which removed all mention of particular religions in Article 44, was supported by 721,003 votes (84.4 per cent) to 133,430. Almost certainly, the fact of there being two ballot papers, albeit in different colours, accounted for the large spoiled vote which, at over 5 per cent, was far above that recorded earlier in the year at the E.E.C. referendum (0.8 per cent). The size of the spoiled vote on this occasion, which confirms the experience in 1959 when the referendum was linked with a presidential election (4.0 per cent) and in 1969 when the proposal involved two ballots (4.3 per cent), suggests that when there is any sort of complication one voter in twenty is liable to waste his vote.

The proposal to lower the minimum voting age to eighteen was originally made to the Committee on the Constitution (1966-7) but that body made no recommendations, having discovered that twice as many countries had a mimimum age of twenty-one as had eighteen and that this majority included, as Deputy Fitzpatrick later put it, 'certain highly respected democracies'. By 1972 all parties had come to favour eighteen and, indeed, at the second stage debate in the Dáil members vied one with another in claiming that it was *their* party that had first proposed it.

In contrast to its equivocation on votes at eighteen, the Committee on the Constitution recommended unanimously that subsections 2 and 3 of Article 44.1 should be deleted. These were the sections which recognized named religions and the first of which, it was claimed, gave the Catholic Church a 'special position'. They ran as follows:

> 2° The State recognises the special position of the Holy Catholic Apostolic and Roman Church as the guardian of the faith professed by the great majority of the citizens.
>
> 3° The State also recognises the Church of Ireland, the Presbyterian Church in Ireland, the Methodist Church in Ireland, the Religious Society of Friends in Ireland, as well as the Jewish Congregations and the other religious denominations existing in Ireland at the date of the coming into operation of this Constitution.

Whatever the motives of those who drafted these provisions and of those who subsequently enacted them, and however they were construed in the forties and fifties, by the late sixties the committee found that

> the general view of commentators on the Constitution is . . . that these provisions are of no juridical effect and do not give any special privilege to the Catholic Church under the Constitution. The prevailing view is that sub-section 2° merely recognizes the statistical fact that the Catholic Church is the guardian of the Faith professed by the great majority of the citizens; other provisions (in Article 44 and elsewhere) of the Constitution prohibit religious discrimination of any kind so that there can be no preference for any particular religion. Not only legal experts but Catholic theologians support this view.

Examination of documents published by and in connection with the Second Vatican Council convinced the committee that 'the Catholic Church does not seek any special recognition or privilege.'[32] Since, also, there was 'no doubt that these provisions give offence to non-catholics and are also a useful weapon in the hands of those who are anxious to emphasise the differences between North and South', the committee felt that sub-section 2° 'might profitably be deleted'. Because sub-section 3° could be held to be restrictive by naming religions it, too, should go. Their deletion 'would also help to promote ecumenism', one of the four reasons given by the Vatican Council for its *Declaration on Religious Freedom.*[33]

Civil disorder in the North from 1969 might have been expected to add urgency to this matter in the South. Cardinal Conway, Archbishop of Armagh and Primate of All Ireland, evidently thought so for in September 1969 he said in answer to a question,

> I personally would not shed a single tear if the relevant sub-sections of Article 44 were to disappear. It confers no legal privilege whatever on the Catholic Church and, if the way to convince our fellow Christians in the North about this is to remove it, then it might be worth the expense of a referendum.[34]

This 'clearance' (as one might think) notwithstanding, it was not until November, 1972 that the Fifth Amendment Bill was introduced into the Dáil.

The Fifth Amendment of the Constitution Bill, 1972, proposed simply that sections 2 and 3 of Article 44.1 be deleted. The ensuing debates and campaign stressed the importance of the change as a contribution to removing misconceptions held in the North and elsewhere about the nature of the Irish Republic and, thus, to eventual Irish unity. Speakers from all parties insisted that the existing provisions were otiose. The change 'has our support mainly because we think it should never have been in the Constitution' Cosgrave declared;[35] it had been a Fianna Fáil mistake in 1937 to depart from the more liberal text of Article 8 of the Irish Free State Constitution. 'A wholly unnecessary irritant which has given to the opponents of this state a stick with which to beat it', said Deputy Richie Ryan: the change should be made not only because of the North but because 'it is good in itself to make it.'[36] Labour, its spokesman claimed, had sought the change for some time.

There was a disposition to go further: spokesmen of all parties urged the need for an entirely new Constitution. A Constitution 'can be Christian without all this effusive, ecclesiastical moralising of the present Constitution of the Republic. That is why we in Fine Gael urge that the present Constitution should be scrapped at the earliest possible date and replaced by a modern, more efficient and honest document.'[37] Although most did not put it as strongly as Richie Ryan, the sense of the Dáil debate was clear: this measure was to be a first instalment.

However, this 'symbolic act', as Erskine Childers called it'[38] did arouse some opposition from more conservative Catholic elements. A 'Defend 44 Campaign', mounted by Mr. D. Broadberry got some publicity but little overt support, though there was reference in the press to a whispering campaign by some Dublin clergy.[39] With one or two exceptions, the Bishops were strangely silent. The Rev. Vincent Kavanagh, Director of the Limerick Archconfraternity voiced publicly what might have been thought by some clergy, and perhaps said by them in private, when he declared:

> I'm opposed to these changes because they are opening the door to all kinds of frightening possibilities. When we allow minorities to bring about changes in our Constitution, the most frightening things can happen.

The Government he thought was using the Catholic Church 'for political gimmickry.'[40]

It was one of the senior Bishops, Bishop Lucey of Cork and Ross, who seems to have been the most important opponent of the bill, certainly in terms of political influence. A week before polling day an editorial in *The Fold,* the Cork diocesan magazine, came out against the change. Since this was generally taken as reflecting the attitude of Dr. Lucey, it was 'accepted by many voters as a guideline' according to a correspondent in the *Irish Times*.[41] But how many? For once it is possible to hazard a rough answer. Over the whole country, the vote in favour of the change was 84.3 per cent. In every constituency save four the percentage in favour was over 81 per cent (varying between 81 per cent and 91 per cent). Of the four, Cork City North West (71.1 per cent), Cork City South East (72.4 per cent) and, Cork South West (76.3 per cent), were in the Sees of Cork and Ross. The other was Limerick East (74.7 per cent), a constituency that includes Limerick City where the Rev. Kavanagh's views, quoted above, perhaps reflected the tone of the clergy and which, in any case, is a city that in the past has sometimes displayed signs of zealous catholicism.

Landslide vote in favour as this was, these interventions made no difference. However, when, as it might appear, a lead from a bishop, even one in such an inauspicious situation as Dr. Lucey found himself – with the Cardinal on the record in favour and in the Taoiseach's own home territory – is worth over ten per cent of the vote, further moves to make the Constitution more acceptable to Northern Protestants by tampering with the Catholic articles would clearly be a hazardous undertaking. Besides, the church was soon to make it clear that for the moment at least 'enough is enough'. For all the politicians' talk about the need for an entirely new constitution, the *Irish Times* was unwittingly right when it concluded its referendum results report on 9 December 1972 with the sentence: 'The ball is now in the *net* of the Constitution Committee.' (Author's italics) The ball was in the net all right, but for quite a different reason, as we shall see in Chapter 10.

Chapter 8

JUDICIAL INTERPRETATION

It should not be imagined that constitutions can be changed only by amending them. There is another important procedure to be considered in this respect, namely judicial interpretation. Courts of law can acquire the role of constitutional developers where they have the legal power to review, that is 'the power . . . to invalidate on constitutional grounds any act of any governmental agency – legislative, executive, administrative, police or judicial.'[1] As Carter and Herz point out, where the courts do have such a power, they deal with three types of cases: first, cases of conflict between public authorities and individuals or groups over alleged violations of rights; second, cases involving the constitutionality of ordinary legislation; and, third, cases involving the proper spheres of action of the organs of government.[2]

Irish courts do have review powers: to be more precise, the High Court and the Supreme Court have such powers.[3] They are either stated in the Constitution or inferred by the courts themselves. The power to review legislation is explicitly stated. Article 15.4.1° forbids the Oireachtas from enacting any law repugnant to the Constitution and, in Article 34.3.2°, the jurisdiction of the High Court is stated as extending 'to the question of the validity of any law having regard to the provisions of the Constitution.' Under Article 34.3.3°, such questions may go on appeal to the Supreme Court. The Supreme Court also has the duty to consider bills referred to it by the President under Article 26 to establish 'whether such Bill or any specified provision or provisions of such Bill is or are repugnant to this Constitution or to any provision thereof.' If the English and Irish texts should conflict, the Irish text prevails (Article 25.5.4°).

According to Article 34.4.5° the decision of the Supreme Court in cases involving 'the validity of a law having regard to the provisions of this Constitution' must be delivered by one judge and 'no other opinion on such question, whether assenting or dissenting, shall be pronounced, nor shall the existence of any such other opinion be disclosed.' This prohibition, added as an amendment to the Constitution in 1942, is according to Heuston, 'contrary to the principles of judicial precedent adopted elsewhere in the common law world.'[4] Perhaps the Supreme Court itself takes this view for it has gone some way to minimize the scope of the provision by delivering multiple judgements in cases where the constitutionality of pre-1937 legislation was in question.[5]

The powers of the High Court and the Supreme Court to invalidate laws are not absolute. If, in a time of war or armed rebellion as defined in Article 28.3.3°, the Oireachtas has resolved that a 'national emergency' exists, no law 'expressed to be for the purpose of securing the public safety and the preservation of the state' can be invalidated. The considerable extent to which this clause can be, and has been, used to preclude judicial review has been explored in Chapter 6 (see p. 50 above).

Power to review the constitutionality of the activities of the government and public authorities can also be regarded as flowing from Article 15 for, it is argued, if the courts have the power to review legislation, it follows that they must also have the power to review what is done under that legislation. In any case, such powers are regarded by lawyers as inherent in the courts. Such powers were vested in British courts and lawyers regard them as having been transferred by way of the Constitution to the appropriate institutions. Limitations on these powers, also inherited, which arose from the presumed transfer to the Irish government of prerogative powers have been removed in recent years by the courts themselves (see p. 77 below).

The power of the High Court and the Supreme Court to *review* for constitutionality obviously gives them the opportunity to *interpret* the Constitution, but in what, if any, sense can they *change* it? Wheare answers the question in this way:

> Courts, it must be emphasized, cannot amend a Constitution. They cannot change the words. They must accept the words, and so far as they introduce change, it can come only through their interpretation of the meaning of the words. Courts may, by a series of decisions, elaborate the content of a word or phrase; they may even revoke or contradict previous decisions. But throughout they are confined to the words of the Constitution. It is true that these words may sometimes be vague or ambiguous, leaving room for judges to supply from their own minds

what the framers of the Constitution might or might not have said . . .[6]

Heuston, however, goes further. He has discerned in the Irish experience 'two distinct modes or techniques' of interpretation, a literal one according to which 'the Constitution must be interpreted from within its own four corners', and 'a very broad approach' which permits reference to the preamble, to Article 45 (the Directive Principles), to the nature of the Irish state, even in the words of Chief Justice O'Higgins in 1976, to 'concepts of prudence, justice and charity which may gradually change or develop as society changes and develops, and which fall to be interpreted from time to time in accordance with prevailing ideas.'[7]

Whatever the grounds upon which courts come to their decisions, it seems obvious that they can, if they will, adapt the meaning of words that purport to define the extent of powers or prohibitions so as to meet the demands of changed circumstances as they see them. Such adaptations might over time completely alter the powers and limitations of governments and the liberties of the citizens as is evidenced, for example, by the history of the interpretation by the Supreme Court of the United States of the power of Congress to regulate inter-state commerce.[8] To the extent that courts do this successfully, it will be unnecessary formally to amend the Constitution. Thus, the power to review is an important device to obtain flexibility and to accommodate social, economic and cultural change, though it has potential dangers and is open to powerful objections, as we shall see.

Examination of the record of the Irish courts shows that there have been two distinct phases; the first, from 1938 to the middle sixties; the second, from the middle sixties onwards. In the first, the courts took up a cautious, even inhibited, approach; in the second, there was a sudden burst of creativity extending over a decade or so.

There is general agreement among the legal writers on this subject that the courts originally took up what McWhinney described as 'a narrow rather inflexible approach to constitutional interpretation, with emphasis on harsh construction and reading down of the constitutional provisions in question.' They were 'rarely innovatory'.[9] Beth described the Irish judges of the period as tending 'to tiptoe around judicial review.'[10]

This diffidence is easily explained. To begin with, the Constitution itself is ambivalent as Beth pointed out. He thought that those who created the Constitution were obviously undecided whether to plump for limited government based on court-enforced constitutional guarantees or for parliamentary supremacy limited only by the respect of political leaders for the Constitution. 'In the event they did neither, and . . . spent thirty years uneasily between the two, like a slack wire performer in a circus.'[11] De Valera's own firmly expressed reservations about the role of the courts have already been mentioned (see p. 51 above). They were widely shared, not least by the legal profession. Barrington thought that 'the general body of the Irish legal profession – both judges and practitioners – appear to have been slow to appreciate the significance of having a written constitution with a charter of rights and judicial review of legislation . . .'[12]

This was natural enough, for the lawyers of that generation – and indeed of the next – were trained in the British tradition with its emphasis on the common law, on the sovereignty of parliament and on judicial precedent, all doctrines to make a conservative judiciary exceedingly chary of putting to creative use the new powers suddenly bestowed upon them, let alone of adopting what McWhinney called 'a policy-oriented approach' in the manner of American judges. Perhaps also, as Kelly has suggested:

> It is difficult properly to appreciate the attitude of the judiciary in this period without understanding that to some of them at least their background and traditions made the very existence of an independent Irish state seem a perilous experiment, and the works and pomps of that state – whether declarations of fundamental rights or, at the other extreme, the establishment of a standing military court – the objects of deep suspicion.[13]

Finally, it has to be remembered that the state had been continuously plagued by subversive organizations and was soon once again in a period of emergency when the war in Europe broke out. The exigencies of those days had their effects upon the demeanour of the judges when dealing with matters of security. It was not a propitious time for enlarging the rights of the citizen.

It is not intended here to review systematically the cases that have arisen involving constitutional interpretation. This has been done adequately elsewhere, particularly for the first period, that up to the middle sixties.[14] The principal features of this period are clear enough. First, there were comparatively few cases of any significance. The legal profession, as Barrington observed, was slow to recognize the opportunities available – they were later to show signs of being as slow to make use of the law of the E.E.C. – and, as Beth pointed out, there was no tradition of private citizens instituting court cases on constitutional points. The plaintiff in *O'Donovan* v. *Attorney General* in 1961 was the first private citizen to take this road. In *The Development of Judicial Review in Ireland, 1937-1966,* Beth analyses the sixty-nine cases involving constitutional interpretation that arose between 1938 and 1966 and shows that as many as twenty-three involved judgements of unconstitutionality. These figures show how important is the power of judicial review and they underline the significance of the High Court and the Supreme Court as political institutions. However, Beth noted that all but eight of these twenty-three findings of unconstitutionality involved 'old laws or rules of common law, in many cases archaic, and certainly developed without any regard to questions of constitutional validity.'[15]

The second feature of the period up to the middle sixties concerns an area of the Constitution that gave rise to important cases in this period, namely personal rights. Here, the courts tended to interpret the rights of the citizen narrowly and to give the legislature and the government considerable powers and discretion. In giving its opinion that a section of the Offences against the State (Amendment) Bill, 1940, that had been challenged did not breach Article 40.3 – the article that binds the state by its laws to respect and so far as practicable by its laws to defend the personal rights of the citizen – the Supreme Court declared that

> the duty of determining the extent to which the rights of any particular citizen, or class of citizens, can properly be harmonized with the rights of the citizens as a whole seems to us to be a matter which is peculiarly within the province of the Oireachtas, and any attempt by this Court to control the Oireachtas in the exercise of this function would, in our opinion, be a usurpation of its authority.[16]

In the same spirit, the phrase 'in accordance with the law', used in a number of articles in the Constitution, was interpreted as meaning 'in accordance with the law as it exists at the time when the particular Article is invoked.' Similarly, in considering the effect of Article 28.3.3° – the article that confers wide powers upon the Oireachtas in times of emergency – the Court gave the executive 'the broad [use] of executive power substantially unfettered by court control.'[17]

Thirdly, in respect of matters such as economic rights, the courts up to the mid-sixties generally held the view that in interpreting the Constitution they should take up a legalistic approach. It was not for them, they thought, to attempt to define, for example, what 'social justice' would require. 'I cannot define that phrase as a matter of law', declared Mr. Justice Hanna and, he went on,

> in a court of law it seems to me to be a nebulous phrase, involving no question of law for the court, but questions of ethics, morals, economics,

> and sociology, which are, in my opinion, beyond the determination of a Court of Law . . .

Like his colleagues, he believed that these were matters 'within the consideration of the Oireachtas, as representing the people, when framing the law.'[18]

Finally, it should be noticed that, during this period, this diffidence extended to a great extent also to the interpretation of the particularly Catholic articles of the Constitution, which were amongst its most novel features and, one might think, bound to invite exegesis. True, some judges did begin to face up to the discrepancies between inherited British law and the Catholic principles of some of the rights articles. Nevertheless, we find the Supreme Court deliberately curbing what McWhinney dubbed 'the comprehensiveness and sweep' of the conclusions drawn by Mr. Justice Gavan Duffy (one of the few innovators on the Bench) from his observation that 'the Irish code marks a new departure from time-honoured precedents.' Consequently, as McWhinney concluded, 'the impact of modern Catholic political, social, and economic ideas on legal development was rather less significant or substantial than the adoption of the radically new Constitution of 1937 might have seemed at the time to foreshadow.'[19]

However, Gavan Duffy was right: 1937 *was* 'a new departure'; but take-off was delayed a while in the case of the courts. By 1967, however, Kelly thought that 'judicial interpretation of the Constitution has been becoming increasingly bold', and he felt able to assert that de Valera had 'underestimated the Fundamental Rights Articles as a check on the legislative power.'[20] Writing in the same year Beth, too, noted a change in the 'restraintist' line hitherto taken by the courts: there was now 'a strong tendency for Irish judges to rethink this matter.'[21] A number of writers have pointed to the judgement in the case of *Ryan* v. *Attorney General*[22] as marking the change. Certainly it seems to have opened up the floodgates so far as the definition of human rights is concerned.

The courts were not alone in shrugging off torpor. The change in their demeanour was but one facet of what Charles McCarthy has dubbed the 'decade of upheaval', for the sixties were years of considerable social, economic and cultural change in Ireland as the country dragged itself out of the stagnation of the post second world war de Valera period.[23] By this time, too, the legal profession was more familiar with the new constitutional situation, having been brought up with it. Concepts of fundamental law were no longer foreign to their training and tradition. The efflux of time brought new men to the High Court and the Supreme Court, some of them lawyers of distinction and originality in the eyes of their peers. By about 1970, Irish lawyers were talking of a three to two majority of 'liberal' or 'progressive' judges in the Supreme Court, and the Court seems to have retained this profile.[24] To a considerable extent this period seems to have coincided with Cearbhall Ó Dálaigh's tenure of office as Chief Justice and President of the Supreme Court.

Increasingly judges, or at least some judges, became more prone to take the broader approach to interpreting the Constitution that Heuston spoke of (see p. 73 above), and to look more widely for guidance as to what the law should be than their predecessors had. Recourse began to be had to the Preamble to the Constitution and to Article 45 (the Directive Principles of Social Policy). In a number of judgements delivered in the early seventies, it was held that these principles, hitherto generally reckoned not to be cognizable by the courts, could be appealed to in certain circumstances, for it is in relation only to the making of laws that the constitutional prohibition on the courts recognizing them applies.[25] Going wider, some judges began to infer from the wording and the general tenor of the Constitution what the Supreme Court called 'basic doctrines of political and social theory.'[26]

The section of the Constitution that seems to have been most substantially developed in recent years is the fundamental rights section, using Article 40.3 as the basis for a concept of 'undisclosed human rights'. As early as 1967, Beth noted that 'Mr. Justice Kenny . . . has been a leader in this movement, but it has secured surprising support from his brethren.'[27] The seminal judgement was that in the case of *Ryan* v. *Attorney General,* to which reference has already been made. In giving judgement, Mr. Justice Kenny discussed Article 40.3 and gave it as his opinion that 'the personal rights which may be invoked to invalidate legislation are not confined to those specified in Article 40 but include all those rights which result from the Christian and democratic nature of the State.'[28]

The implications of this line of approach are enormous. By 1974 Mr. Justice Walsh was arguing (in *McGee* v. *Attorney General*) that

> Articles 41, 42 and 43 emphatically reject the theory that there are no rights without laws, no rights contrary to the law and no rights anterior to the law. They indicate that justice is placed above the law and acknowledge that natural rights or human rights are not created by law but that the Constitution can confirm their existence and give them protection.[29]

'The speed with which new unspecified rights can be recognized and enforced is startling', Heuston thought.[30] He listed nine, among them the right to bodily integrity, the right to work, the right to belong to a trade union, the right to a career, the right to free movement and the right to marry.[31]

The same avenue was also used to broaden the access to the courts. Beth was right when he anticipated that Article 40.3 would form 'the basis for a concept of "natural justice" which may some day serve effectively as an Irish counterpart of due process, at least in trial rights cases.'[32] Since 1965 there have been a number of important cases; among them *The State (Quinn)* v. *Ryan and Others* which, among other things, concerned the right of unhampered access to the courts to question the validity of a warrant; *Macauley* v. *The Minister for Posts and Telegraphs* in which it was held that the necessity to have the *fiat* of the Attorney General in order to proceed against a minister impeded the right of recourse to the courts; and *Byrne* v. *Ireland and the Attorney General* which dealt with the question of the right of a citizen to sue the state for a civil wrong.[33]

It is obvious from these examples of the courts' activities and others like them that the Constitution offers considerably more scope than was earlier thought possible or appropriate for judges to increase and enlarge the rights of the citizen and to make positive and far-reaching contributions to the corpus of law. Heuston wondered whether, in extending the sources to which they were prepared to look for guidance and in the construction they put upon what they found, they had not already gone 'to the furthest limit of judicial lawmaking.'[34] Although they are never likely to emulate their American brothers in law or to take up so overtly political a stance, they have already gone far enough for doubts to have been raised about the wisdom of their invading the political domain. As Heuston has remarked, 'it is surprising to find so little political enmity towards the courts on the part of members of the Oireachtas or administrators, because many of the court's decisions . . . have been exceedingly inconvenient from an administrative point of view.'[35]

There is here a real dilemma. On the one hand, there is obvious value in having the courts flesh out the Constitution and adapt it to changing conditions and community values: on the other hand, there is a very real danger of uncertainty as to what the law is if the courts are going to continue to extend the scope of Article 40.3, seemingly without end. There is danger, too, of hostility if they come to act as a 'third house of the legislature' testing legislation against 'their own criteria of wisdom and policy', as Kelly put it.[36] In countries where the courts have taken an active role in developing the Constitution, they are often forced into adopting what McWhinney called 'a policy-oriented approach'[37] for which, as some might think, they are not well fitted and which can lead to threats to that insulation from politics which in many respects is an essential feature of the Judiciary. As Wheare asks, 'why should judges be thought more trustworthy than legislators or administrators?'[38]

De Valera's strong views upon this subject have already been mentioned (p. 51 above) and, though he spoke in a particular context, the ever-present danger is obvious. It is of damage to the courts whenever they come to be suspected of usurping functions that many think are proper to the Oireachtas. Criticism of this sort inevitably brings the judges into public controversy; 'it means, too, that their appointments are criticized and canvassed';[39] and it focuses attention upon who the judges are and how they are appointed. In these respects they do not stand up well to the scrutiny of an increasingly egalitarian community for they cannot by a long chalk be called 'representative' in any of the many meanings of that elusive term. As Loewenstein has remarked, 'basically the independence of the judiciary resolves itself into the sociological dilemma of a judicial caste.'[40] In this day and age it is not possible for such a caste to have too prominent a role without suffering attack.

If, as seems to be the case, the courts in interpreting the Constitution are having an important and growing effect upon the law, this is likely to be matched, in some respects even overshadowed, by the impact of new sources of law upon the extension of rights and the imposition of duties. Beyond the domestic law of Ireland and its indigenous sources, there now stretch the vast expanses of the law of the European Communities, a territory as yet hardly explored by the Irish. It is to this law that we now turn.

Chapter 9

THE CONSTITUTION AND MEMBERSHIP OF THE EUROPEAN COMMUNITIES

Ireland's accession to the European Communities in January 1972 brought the state into 'a new type of international organization with much greater powers over member countries than those traditionally given to international institutions.'[1] Membership of the Communities – the European Economic Community (the Treaty of Rome, 1957), the European Atomic Energy Community (the Treaty of Rome, 1957) and the European Coal and Steel Community (the Treaty of Paris, 1951) – which in common parlance are often called simply but inaccurately 'the E.E.C.' – imposes obligations and confers rights not only in the treaties themselves, but also by virtue of what the members have wished upon themselves since they came together through the various organs of the Communities. When Ireland joined the Communities, it came into a polity with fifteen years of activity behind it. In principle at least, the law of the European Communities had to be received into Irish law, though transitional arrangements, derogations and simple inertia have dragged out, and continue to drag out, the process of reception.

A potent source of law such as the Communities could hardly fail to have an impact upon the Constitution. A constitutional amendment was needed before Ireland could join at all; and the factual position since accession being in some respects at variance with what is stated in the Constitution, a number of others are desirable if not absolutely necessary. The potential effects of membership of an institution that can create rights and obligations as the Communities can are almost incalculable. Lord Justice Denning described the impact of Community law as 'like an incoming tide. It flows into the estuaries and up the rivers. It cannot be held back.' His description can be as aptly applied to Ireland as to the U.K. (the context in which he made it[2]).

Countries like France, Germany and Italy which had made fresh starts after the second world war reflected in their new post-war constitutions the strong disposition of continental western European political leaders to qualify the concept of sovereignty. Reviewing them, Carl J. Friedrich thought that 'perhaps the most novel aspect of these constitutions is their abandonment of national sovereignty as a central presupposition of their political theory.'[3] In such a political climate and with appropriately conceived basic law, it was not difficult for these countries to accommodate to a European Community.

Ireland, by contrast, has a pre-war constitution and unlike the states of continental western Europe has enjoyed unbroken political stability since its inception. It is not surprising that Bunreacht na hÉireann, framed as it was in the middle thirties, did not fit Ireland to enter a political organization like the Community, for it belonged to an era that did not comtemplate such a political entity. The Constitution reflects the 'dualist' approach to the relationship between international law and domestic law. The basic principle of the dualist approach is that there are two separate and quite distinct legal systems: one regulates relations between states, the other between persons in a state. They are different in subject matter and content.

Article 29.6 of the Constitution 'explicitly lays down a "dualist" approach to international law.'[4] It requires that the state shall determine for itself how and to what extent it will receive international law.

> No international agreement shall be part of the domestic law of the State save as may be determined by the Oireachtas.

During the late sixties, when Ireland was for the second time an applicant for membership of the Communities, the constitutional difficulties involved were teased out by lawyers and civil servants. One of those involved, John Temple Lang, summed them up in this way:

> Since the Community Treaties must be received into Irish law by an Act of the Irish legislature, the provisions of the Treaties cannot become part of Irish law unless they are consistent with the provisions of the Irish Constitution. As it is at present the Irish Constitution does not allow the legislature to confer on the Community institutions *the powers which belong to them under the Treaties,* so as to make these powers effective under Irish law.[5] (author's italics)

'The powers which belong to them under the Treaties': these are the significant words. Article 29.6 of the Constitution is adequate for situations in which the state assumes ordinary treaty obligations, including treaties of the convention kind that purport to create human rights. (The European Convention on Human Rights to which Ireland subscribes is one of these.) Such treaties might impose an obligation upon a country to alter its domestic law, but such action is entirely a matter for government and parliament. (In fact, Ireland still has to alter certain of its laws to accord with that Convention.) They might also include arrangements by which states bind themselves in advance to accept the jurisdiction of judicial institutions and even to allow individual citizens to proceed against states, as the European Convention does, but these are matters entirely for states to decide for themselves. Those who signed the Treaties of Rome and Paris, however, were doing much more than this. Those Treaties

> . . . created an entirely new order of international law.
>
> Under international law, as it is normally understood, only states can be bound by international treaties. The originality of Community law stems from the fact that much of it applies directly to the individual citizen, imposing clearly-defined obligations as well as granting certain rights. These rights and obligations must be upheld in the first instance by national courts and in the second instance by the European Court of Justice.[6]

Thus the Communities can alter national law directly by creating rules of law that have immediate validity without any need for approval by national parliaments. Community *regulations* and *decisions* are instruments of this kind, being directly applicable in the member states and binding all to whom they apply including public authorities themselves. The rights and obligations they create must be upheld both by national courts and by the Communities' judicial organ, the European Court of Justice. *Directives,* on the other hand, which are the usual means of requiring states to harmonize their laws, do not themselves become part of national law. However, they do impose upon the states to which they are addressed an obligation 'to bring about a specified result, but the choice of form and methods of carrying out directives is left to the national authorities.'[7]

The need to amend the Constitution in order to permit Ireland to join was generally acknowledged by the middle sixties. A Government White Paper in 1970 listed both a number of provisions of the Constitution that would 'have to be considered' were Ireland to join and also provisions of the E.E.C. Treaty that 'could be held to be inconsistent with' or 'in conflict with' the Constitution as it stood. It recognized also that 'amendments to our domestic legislation would be necessary.' A committee was already examining the 'changes which would be required in our domestic laws in order to adapt them to the provisions of the Treaties and action taken in implementation of these provisions.'[8]

Instead of making a whole series of changes in the Constitution, which would have been an uncertain, complicated and messy business, it was decided to insert a single new section into the Constitution that would enable Ireland to join and would provide that no legislation on actions needed to give effect to Community measures could be invalidated by reason of unconstitutionality. Accordingly, the Third Amendment of the Constitution Act, agreed to in a referendum in May 1972, added one sub-section to Article 29.4. (For the text of the amendment, see p. 65 above).

The way was now clear for an accession act. In fact, the treaty of accession had already been signed in January.[9] It was to take effect from 1 January 1973; though not full effect, for a number of interim arrangements were included in the treaty. The necessary act, the European Communities Act, 1972 (No. 27) completed the process. It provided that from 1 January 1973

> the Treaties governing the European Communities and the existing and future acts adopted by the institutions of those communities shall be binding on the state and shall be part of the domestic law thereof under the conditions laid down in those treaties. (Section 2)

It also empowered ministers to make regulations to enable section 2 of the act 'to have full effect.' The government is required to make a report twice yearly to each house of the Oireachtas 'on developments in the European Communities.' These reports, intended to give the Oireachtas information and to provide material for debate, have evoked little enough interest and very few of them have been debated. In the Spring of 1977 the Dáil had not had a debate on them for two years and the Seanad since the previous Spring.[10]

Given the aims of the European Communities and the powers of their institutions, in particular the Council, the Commission and the Court, they could not but have a big impact upon the domestic law of the members relating to the matters covered by the Treaties. The Communities were set up not only to make future war between the members impossible but also to forge economic ties and create economic conditions that would generate growing prosperity, as well as to improve the living and working conditions of community citizens. Later, as complete economic unity was foreseen and perhaps also, ultimately, political unity, social aims were enlarged and emphasised. 'Economic expansion is not an end in itself', the leaders of the nine member states declared in Paris in 1972; 'it should result in an improvement in the quality of life as well as in standards of living.' In order to achieve these aims, it was recognized from the beginning that the laws of the member states relating to matters covered in the Treaties would have to be harmonized and Article 100 of the Treaty of Rome gives the Council powers to effect what it calls 'approximation'. It soon came to be realized also that Community law would have to prevail over national law. The Treaties did not state this clearly and unequivocally, but the European Court of Justice has gone far to establish it.

Although the economic and social matters that are the concern of the Communities hardly touch upon family law, they do subsume such areas as social welfare and such personal rights as sex equality, equal pay, the right to work, and freedom of establishment. It is most obviously matters such as these, as also the rights and powers of the Communities' institutions, that impinge upon the Constitution and raise questions about the need for constitutional amendment. It has to be recognized, however, that it is impossible to be precise about the constitutional implications of Ireland's obligations as a member. Because the Communities are making rules all the time, questions could arise in respect of any of the matters covered by the Treaties and perhaps some that, though they are not explicitly mentioned, might be inferred.

The way to Ireland's accession was cleared by means of the addition of a single section to Article 29. This was no doubt the neatest, and certainly the simplest, method. However, the result of proceeding in this manner is that the factual position in respect of a number of matters dealt with in the Constitution is not what the Constitution says it is. To a layman at least, there appear to be internal inconsistencies if not contradictions in the text.

This situation arises even as a consequence of the insertion of subsection 29.4.3° (the Third Amendment) itself. With that section, which establishes the supremacy of Community law, the dualist approach explicitly enshrined in Article 29.6 no longer obtains in respect of part of Irish law, namely those areas covered by the Treaties.

Again, by joining the Communities, Ireland received and has continued to receive a great amount of law that has not been passed by the Oireachtas. Some of it is of direct effect once made by Community institutions. For the rest, governments are bound to take steps to implement it. Article 189 of the Treaty of Rome establishing the E.E.C. is explicit on this matter:

> In order to carry out their task the Council and the Commission shall, in accordance with the provisions of this Treaty, make regulations, issue directives, take decisions, make recommendations or deliver opinions.
>
> A regulation shall have general application. It shall be binding in its entirety and directly applicable in all Member States.
>
> A directive shall be binding, as to the result to be achieved, upon each Member State to which it is addressed, but shall leave to the national authorities the choice of form and methods.
>
> A decision shall be binding in its entirety upon those to whom it is addressed.

Under section 2 of the European Communities Act, 1972, ministers have the power to make regulations to give effect to these obligations. There are, however, statements in the Constitution that appear to say something very different, though they are of course negatived by Article 29.4.3°. Notably, Article 15.2 vests in the Oireachtas 'the sole and exclusive power of making laws for the State' and provides that 'no other legislative authority has power to make laws for the State.' In 1970, the Government thought that this and other provisions of the sort in the Constitution would 'have to be considered in this regard.'[11] This is still very much the case.

The impact of Community law upon Irish law and the actions of the Irish government is considerable though, as yet, largely unrecognized. Surveying the situation in the Spring of 1977, an Oireachtas committee

> [doubted] if the general public or even parliamentarians appreciate the extent to which Community law which governs activities in the fields of trade, industry, transport, agriculture and services, is continuously being incorporated into our legal system either directly or through the agency of statutory instruments made by Ministers.[12]

In the opinion of some lawyers, a number of acts on the Irish statute book might well be open to challenge by reference to Community law and require amendment. There is much more to come, for one of the major aims of the E.E.C. is to harmonize the laws of the members. The harmonization of company law that is under way at present will, when the directives are adopted, necessitate considerable changes in Irish statutes, including the Companies Act, 1963.[13] Some of the considerable number of changes in Irish labour law made in 1977 were directly required by E.E.C. directives. The Federated Union of Employers informed its members that 'both the *Protection of Employment Act, 1977* and the *Employment Equality Act, 1977* follow directly from, and bear a very close similarity with, two

E.E.C. Directives on Collective Dismissals and Equality of Treatment.'[14] It expected more such enforced changes, particularly in regard to safety at work.

The effect that Community law can have upon government policy was well illustrated in 1976 in the matter of equal pay. Having first apparently misinterpreted its obligations in respect of equal pay (laid down in Article 119 of the Treaty of Rome and in Directive 75/117/EEC), the Government first tried unsuccessfully to obtain a derogation from them, but, in May 1976, embarrassed and irritated, it abandoned a bill intended to amend the Anti-Discrimination (Pay) Act, 1974, then at second stage in the Dáil.[15]

Clearly, the Oireachtas is very far from having 'the sole and exclusive power of making laws for the State.' This is not to say that it does not make an effort 'to retain some influence in those areas in which legislative competence was ceded to the Community institutions on our accession.'[16] There exists a 'Joint Committee [of the Dáil and Seanad] on the Secondary Legislation of the European Communities' whose terms of reference are to examine and report on proposals made by the Commission to the Council of Ministers for legislation (regulations, directives etc.), on acts of the Community institutions, and on Irish statutory instruments (ministerial regulations) implementing Community legislation. The committee is concerned to investigate the effect of Community legislation on Irish law and its implications for Ireland generally. Irish members of the European Parliament are members of the committee *ex officio* and, although they have not been able to attend frequently enough for them to contribute to its work, they do get briefed on proposals coming before the European Parliament.

After a slow start, the committee worked quite effectively at least in so far as it provided a check on the propensity of some departments to abuse their rule-making power under the European Communities Act, 1972, and operated a screening and publicity service for the Oireachtas. In the two years from Summer 1975 to Summer 1977 it issued fifty reports: significantly, as the committee itself lamented, 'none of the reports has been discussed in either House.' They had, however, 'been taken into account in Government Departments' and 'there is evidence that it [the Committee] has had an influence on the drafting of domestic statutory instruments.'[17] Considering the range and importance of Community activities, however, a much bigger operation altogether was needed. The incoming Fianna Fáil Government recognized this in 1977 and by early 1978 the committee had been given wider terms of reference and was working in four sub-committees. It remains to be seen whether its reports will receive attention from the Oireachtas.

As with the legislature, so, too, with the judiciary. Article 34.1 of the Constitution provides that 'justice shall be administered in courts established by law by judges appointed in the manner provided by this Constitution . . .' The Court of Justice of the Communities (usually known as the European Court), however, has the function of ensuring that Community law is observed and, as we have seen, that law permeates Irish law. Thus, the European Court stands alongside, and in certain circumstances stands above, the Irish courts.

Under Article 34.4.6° of the Constitution, the decision of the Supreme Court is in all cases 'final and conclusive'. Article 177 of the Rome Treaty, however, provides that where any question involving the validity and interpretation of European Community laws or measures is raised in a case before a domestic court that court may refer, and if it is a final court of appeal, must refer the matter to the European Court. Although the European Court cannot intervene directly in cases before national courts, there is a procedure by which a 'preliminary ruling' can be sought, thus allowing the European Court to interpret the point of Community law involved. The national court is expected to follow the ruling given. In a case involving alleged illegal fishing by Dutch trawlers in 1977, the Cork District Court referred the issue to the European Court. In February, 1978, the Court found that measures taken by the Irish Government to prevent fishing close to its shores 'breached the general non-discrimination rule in Article 7 of the E.E.C. Treaty' and were also contrary to Article 2(1) of Regulation (E.E.C.) no. 101/76.[18]

The supremacy of Community law, not absolutely clear in the beginning, was soon established. In 1972, John Temple Lang thought that

> it could be that Article 189 itself embodies the rule that in all cases of conflict Community law, so far as directly applicable, prevails automatically . . . There is weighty authority for this view in the judgement of the Community Court in the case of *Costa* v *E.N.E.L.* (6/64)[19]

In any case, under Article 171 of the Treaty of Rome, the appropriate Irish authorities are 'bound to take the measures required for the implementation of the judgement of the Court.' Although the Court 'has no physical means of enforcing its judgements', it appears that 'in practice they are never ignored.'[20]

States have in the past been slow to allow their citizens to bring them before international courts. To some people this would be the very negation of the concept of sovereignty. The European Convention on Human Rights does contain such a provision but as an 'optional extra' (to which Ireland subscribes). The member states of the European Communities have, however, surrendered this right for good. Under Article 173 of the Treaty of Rome, 'any natural or legal person' is entitled to have resort to the Court. Not only can Community law be used in the domestic courts, but also the European Court has progressively extended the right of individuals to arraign their public authorities in their domestic courts under European law. The case of *Reyners* v. *Belgian State* established that provisions of the Treaties which are directly applicable 'can be enforced by individuals through the national courts without the interposition of either national legislation or secondary legislation of the Communities.'[21] In the case of *Van Duyn* v. *Home Office* the European Court ruled that 'a provision in a directive imposing obligations on member states can, in some circumstances, be capable of producing direct effects on the legal relation between the member states and individuals and of creating the right for the latter to invoke these obligations in the National Courts.'[22]

The intrusion of European law into the domestic courts and the availability of the European Court, together with the right to bring one's own government before it and before the domestic courts are momentous changes. The Constitution by no means envisages them, much less spells them out. Perhaps it is time it did.

As yet, European law has not been much invoked in the Irish courts and few have had recourse to the European Court. Ireland joined the Communities only in 1973 and most Irish lawyers are still in the process of becoming familiar with a large body of new law. So far, most are not accustomed to look to it or invoke it: it is only a matter of time before they do.

Just as the judges of the Irish courts are extending the rights of Irish citizens by their interpretation of the Constitution, so too the European Court is defining and creating rights, and this aspect of its activities is becoming more and more significant. The Treaties contain no catalogue of human rights though, as the member states move – albeit somewhat haltingly – towards 'European Union', the Commission at least has no doubt but that there will have to be one. Nevertheless, over the years, the Court of Justice has moved inexorably into the field of human rights and has both greatly increased the protection given to the citizen and extended the list.

Generally, the rights affected by the Community are not the classic liberal rights such as belief, conscience, or freedom from arrest; rather it is economic and, increasingly, social rights that are being defined, expanded and enforced. Attention has been paid to such matters as, to name some of the more noteworthy, discrimination on grounds of nationality; equality for the sexes in regard to pay, access to employment, training, promotion; free movement; the right to set up in business or to practise a profession; migrant workers; competition and discrimination against small enterprises.

Like the Irish judges who have looked to sources other than the words of the Constitution, the European Court 'has evolved its case law in a far wider legal framework than that outlined in the Treaties.'[23] In the case of *Internationale Handelsgesellschaft mbH* v. *Einfuhr Vorratsstelle für Getreide und Futtermittel,* the Court declared that 'respect for fundamental rights forms an integral part in the general principles of law for which the Court of Justice ensures respect.' In the case of *Nold J., KG* v. *E.C. Commission,* it felt 'bound to draw inspiration from the constitutional traditions common to the member states' and it looked to the European Convention on Human Rights as a guide.[24]

Welcome though these developments most certainly should be to the citizen, though not always to governments, they do mean that the area of human rights is fast becoming a happy hunting ground for some lawyers and an impenetrable jungle for the rest of us. Obviously, an organic growth of human rights such as occurs when the law is developed in this way is to be welcomed; but, as growth does take place, there is much to be said for an appropriate redefinition of the fundamental rights articles of the Constitution. The rapid burgeoning of human rights in recent years makes such a re-enunciation now overdue.

During the debates preceding the referendum on joining the Communities, much was made of the danger to Irish sovereignty. By joining, it was argued, Ireland would lose her sovereignty or some part of it. From a constitutional point of view, accession to a political organization as powerful as the European Communities might, indeed, seem to put in question the wording of Article 5 which declares that 'Ireland is a sovereign, independent, democratic state.'

'Sovereignty', which is defined in the White Paper of 1970 as 'autonomous powers of decision over domestic and foreign policies',[25] is a very slippery concept, as much political as legal. As the Government saw it then:

> all international cooperation involves some limitation on sovereignty. Even a simple bilateral trade agreement with its reciprocal commitments, places curbs on the freedom of action of the parties. International agreements to which Ireland is a party, such as the General

> Agreement on Tariffs and Trade, the Statute of the Council of Europe, the European Convention on Human Rights or the Charter of the United Nations, place obligations on the participating states, some of which involve substantial derogations from sovereignty.[26]

It can, of course, be argued that at some point in the process of undertaking such obligations and ceding powers of decision to international bodies, the term sovereign becomes inappropriate. In any case, the scope of Community action is wider than, and the nature of the Communities different from, other international co-operative arrangements. What is more, two of the three treaties have no limit: they are 'concluded for an unlimited period' (Treaty of Rome, Article 240). The other, the European Coal and Steel Community Treaty, runs for fifty years. In no case is there a unilateral right of withdrawal. Were a state to denounce them, the European Court would probably hold parties in the denouncing state to be bound in law.

Wide though the scope and broad the powers of the Communities are, they are restricted to economic and social matters. Membership involves, in particular, no military or defence commitments. The aspirations expressed in the Treaty of Rome itself, though, are wide-ranging and the direction of recent developments are significant. The Preamble to the Treaty speaks of the determination of the parties 'to lay the foundations of an ever-closer union among the peoples of Europe.' As the Communities developed, the ambitions of some at least of those who directed its affairs grew. In 1969, the Commission characterized the Treaties of Rome and Paris as 'only one step towards the construction of an increasingly united and institutionalized Europe. The applicant countries [of which Ireland was one] must be fully aware of the fact that they are not only joining an economic and social undertaking, but that they will be required to participate fully in creating a continent which is economically and politically united.'[27]

The heady hopes of the 1960s evaporated somewhat under the stresses of worldwide economic recession. The creation of a monetary union met considerable resistance and, despite the pressure of the Commission, it was clear that 'there was to be no stampede to political union.'[28] Political cooperation was at first pursued outside the Community framework, but gradually the idea of members having common foreign policies began to be realized in small but significant ways. By 1974, there were regular meetings of the foreign ministers of the nine to try to reach common positions on foreign policy issues. Later, heads of government also began to meet regularly. In December 1974, the Minister for Foreign Affairs reported to the Oireachtas that 'it is common practice for the nine to consult with each other before and during meetings of the United Nations General Assembly and international conferences in which all of the member states are participating in order to coordinate positions so far as this is practicable.[29]

By 1975, the Commission, which tends to go somewhat ahead of the member states in these matters, was outlining the indispensable conditions of what by that time was already being called 'European Union'. The Union's competence should embrace defence, foreign policy, and the protection of human rights. The member governments themselves, though, are a long way from desiring, let alone achieving, this. If the nine become the ten, the eleven and so on, it might become even more difficult. In any case, such a 'European Union' would clearly require new legal instruments going far beyond the present treaties, and these would necessitate the approval of each government and parliament and, in most cases, of each people in a referendum.

Might there come a point when the adjective 'sovereign' in Article 5 will be inappropriate? John Temple Lang's answer, given in 1966, is still probably right:

> until further obligations are undertaken by E.E.C. member states, they continue to be independent and sovereign in international law. . . . Since sovereignty is not a precise concept, it is not possible to say exactly at what point in the process of political integration member states would cease to be sovereign, but as long as foreign policy and defence are not assigned, the member states remain sovereign and independent.[30]

During the debates on joining the Communities, the Government and committed pro-Europeans like Dr Garret FitzGerald argued that the hypothetical question of loss of sovereignty was of less importance than the actual opportunity to have a voice, albeit one voice among many, in matters that inevitably were going to affect the country's welfare. The 1972 White Paper expressed that point of view:

> Such limitations on national freedom of action which membership of the Communities will involve for us will be more than counter-balanced by the influence which we will be able to bring to bear on the formulation of Community policies affecting our interests. We must contrast this with our present position as a very small country, independent but with little or no capacity to influence events abroad that significantly affect us.[31]

Although movement towards European union may be slow and there are many hesitations and set-backs, it is hard to avoid the conclusion that the evolution of the Communities will in the end erode the sovereignty of the state. Eventually, the Constitution will have to give legal sanction to the end of what is already a political anachronism. In the circumstances of 1937, it no doubt seemed important to declare that Ireland was a 'sovereign' state: to many today, it does not.

Chapter 10

A CONSTITUTION FOR A UNITED IRELAND?

Whereas the Constitution of the Irish Free State was much amended and became something of a political football, Bunreacht na hÉireann has, so far, been but little changed. Apart from the two amendments occasioned by the second world war, no alterations were formally proposed before 1958-9 and none were actually made until the seventies. For over thirty years, the social and political ideals reflected in the Constitution, the interpretation of Ireland's status embodied in it, and the way in which it dealt with the important and emotive issues evoked by terms such as 'nation', 'national territory' etc., all proved to have been acceptable to the community generally. The principles and institutions of government that the Constitution prescribes, which were largely taken over from the Irish Free State Constitution, further confirmed their suitability. The abortive attempts of Fianna Fáil Governments to amend Article 16 (which deals with elections) showed that, whereas some politicians were anxious to see P.R. replaced by what in their eyes would be a more convenient system, the majority of the electorate not only did not desire this change, but were suspicious of those who did. Thus, Ireland had a basic instrument that stood the test of time.

From the late sixties, however, there was continual talk of amending and, increasingly, of replacing the Constitution. It arose mainly from two causes: first, the fundamental changes that occurred in Europe in the fifties and sixties, not least in the Catholic Church, began to have their impact upon Ireland; second, civil strife in Northern Ireland reopened the border issue that had lain dormant, and brought most people in the Republic to a more realistic appreciation of the true nature of the Northern problem. In particular, there was a growing understanding of the fears and resentment of Northern Ireland Protestants about the Republic's claim to sovereignty over the North and their beliefs about religious and civil liberties in the Republic. There evolved a conjunction of emotive nationalist issues and questions involving the liberalisation and secularisation of the Constitution that has had unfortunate consequences.

From 1969 onwards, the question of amending the Constitution has been (and continues at present to be) discussed almost wholly in the context of the Northern troubles and, increasingly, of a hypothetical united Ireland. Inevitable though discussion in those terms might be, it has had the effect of stultifying change, for the Northern problem remains intractable. Increasingly, as a result, there are signs of frustration among those politicians and opinion leaders who recognize that changes in the social and political climate in western Europe, that are increasingly affecting the Irish people also, urgently need to be reflected in the country's basic law.

At the beginning of this study of Irish constitutions, it was suggested that successive versions reflected above all continuity and development. In many respects Bunreacht na hÉireann did mark progress in Irish political development, but only if viewed from the perspective of *one* of the two communities in Ireland. To nearly everyone in this community, which comprised the majority of the people of Ireland, the only proper end to the process was, and to most of that majority still is, an all-Ireland constitution for an all-Ireland state. What very few in this community saw at the time was that as an attempt at an all-Ireland constitution Bunreacht na hÉireann was both premature and clumsy. Containing as it did some provisions that were wildly inappropriate from the viewpoint of the other, the Northern Protestant, community, it was strongly counter-productive.

Certainly de Valera had an eye upon the North as he drafted it: witness his explanation in the Dáil for not including an explicit declaration that the state was a republic.[1] Nevertheless, as Conor Cruise O'Brien has said,

> if indeed he was interested in wooing 'the North' – in practice, the Protestants of Northern Ireland – his Constitution of 1937 was an odd bouquet to choose.
>
> Article 2 of the Constitution declared the national territory to be 'the whole island of Ireland, its islands and the territorial seas.'
>
> Article 3 asserted – while leaving in suspense for the time being – 'the

> right of the Parliament and Government established by this Constitution to exercise jurisdiction over the whole of that territory.'
>
> Article 44.1.2° recognized 'the special position of the Holy Catholic, Apostolic and Roman Church as the guardian of the Faith professed by the great majority of the citizens.'
>
> Thus, the Protestants of Northern Ireland were declared incorporated *de jure* into a State which recognized the special position of the Roman Catholic Church.
>
> It would be hard to think of a combination of propositions more likely to sustain and stiffen the siege-mentality of Protestant Ulster.[2]

The truth was that de Valera's ideals – and they were accepted by the majority – were mutually exclusive. It was not possible to have a Gaelic, Catholic, thirty-two county republic – even a covert republic. That he cherished *all* of them and claimed to be pursuing them all (though he did not pursue the thirty-two county ideal too actively) can best be explained in Senator Eoin Ryan's words: 'for some reason, Dev. never quite got the wavelength of the North – Unionists or Nationalists.'[3] It is important to make the point that he was by no means alone in this: very few in the South were properly tuned in to the North, at least until the Northern troubles from 1969 onwards.

The mutual incompatibility of Southern ideals was made the greater because of the ready acceptance of contemporary Catholic social teaching. Garret FitzGerald is reported as saying that it was, 'an unfortunate period in history to be drawing it [the Constitution] up because it was a period when a strong view was held that a constitution should incorporate ideas emanating from a particular church. This view wouldn't have been held twenty years earlier or say twenty to thirty years later.'[4] The Constitution, as Professor John A. Murphy put it, 'enshrines what was then a fashionable, but what proved to be a very ephemeral, social ethos. In other words, the notion that you could have a Catholic social order in a state, based on Papal Encyclicals, has now disappeared without trace.'[5] Again, it has to be repeated that it is only recently, to be accurate since Vatican II, that this view became acceptable, let alone gradually accepted. By 1971, however, it was widely enough recognized for politicians to be able to say so in a conservative newspaper like the *Irish Independent:* Bunreacht na hÉireann was, wrote Deputy Richie Ryan,

> a partitionist Constitution . . . an illiberal one . . . It was definitely not the kind of instrument to be the fundamental law of a country which aimed at catering for the different streams of people living in a 32-counties state.[6]

This view is commonplace today. It was by no means so in the late thirties when de Valera could declare that 'we are a Catholic nation'[7] and still be somewhat behind some of Richie Ryan's party forebears in displaying Catholic zeal.

This change in attitude was as sudden as it was extreme. That it was so was due to a coincidence of powerful forces. Its timing was occasioned by the outbreak of the Northern troubles. For de Valera and his followers, the Constitution 'was at once both a constitutional imperative and a document of national philosophy.'[8] While he ruled, it remained so. The only constitutional change, though not literally an amendment of the Constitution, was the Republic of Ireland Act, 1948, and the subsequent declaration of a republic on Easter day 1949. This was a measure, remember, that was carried out by de Valera's opponents and one that underlined the consensus in the twenty-six counties.[9] In their own sphere of interest, the Irish bishops, in this period at their most conservative, held the constitutional position of the church steady and stood four-square over the Catholic rights enshrined therein.

The sixties, however, saw the beginnings of considerable changes in the culture of the Irish. The Republic gradually became a less clerically-dominated, more secular and more liberal society. The change was marked by 'explicit repudiations by Catholics . . . of what had been done in the nineteen forties and fifties.'[10] By 1969, Cardinal Conway was prepared for the removal of the 'special position' article and, though for the moment he drew the line there, the implications for Ireland of the Second Vatican Council were slowly but surely coming to be recognized and accepted. Moreover, as Whyte put it, at that time, 'Ireland as a whole, and not just Irish society in its religious aspect, passed some kind of turning point.'[11] It was becoming industrialized at a faster rate than hitherto and it was getting richer more quickly. With a national television service, the whole country was becoming exposed to metropolitan values; and with the prospect of entering the European Communities, it was more outward looking.

Seán Lemass who, to his credit, recognized the need for matching changes, both of policy and organization, approached the problem of constitutional reform by way of an informal all-party committee. That committee, to whose work attention has already been drawn,[12] not only identified the nature of the changes that were occurring and saw their constitutional implications, but also showed a considerable willingness and ability to grasp nettles. It was able unanimously to recommend rewording for Articles 3 (on the extent of the application of the laws of the state), 41 (on marriage) and 44 (on the recognition of religions and the special position of the Catholic Church). It was, however, ahead of its time; and its members – especially the Fianna Fáil representatives – were certainly ahead of their parties. The committee in any case foundered on the disagreement over P.R. when Fianna Fáil went ahead on its own and attempted to alter the electoral system: with this disagreement went the bilateral approach to constitutional reform.

The eruption of disorder in Northern Ireland 'created . . . a situation in which the whole question of a united Ireland [became] a live issue.'[13] From then on, questions of constitutional change in the Republic were discussed in that context almost exclusively. The Constitution came to be viewed by more and more politicians as an obstacle to unity and proposals to change it were judged on their supposed impact upon Northern opinion. At first, there was a flurry of debate and some activity. In December, 1971, the *Irish Independent* ran a series entitled 'The Constitution – and the Obstacles to Unity.' At a more sophisticated level, Conor Cruise O'Brien in *States of Ireland* (1972) analysed the Irish problem and 'tried to understand some of the feelings shared by most Ulster Protestants and to communicate some notion of these feelings to Catholics in the Republic'[14]: in the course of doing so he exposed the incongruity of Bunreacht na hÉireann for a thirty-two county state. His view, however, that unity was neither likely, nor even widely desired, was – and is – both rejected and resented by many. More in the spirit of the times was Garret FitzGerald's *Towards a New Ireland* (1972) with its outline of changes that would 'have to be made in order to achieve a society which is acceptable to all Irishmen.'[15] Others tried their hands at drafting new constitutions.[16] In that same year, 1972, Article 44 was amended.[17] But that was both the beginning and the end of actual constitutional change: political leaders have made no major, sustained or cooperative efforts since. Why not?

Clearly, the possibilities of changing 'Catholic' articles were to some extent governed by the pace at which the Catholic bishops adopted the more liberal attitudes in regard to the rights and practices of other religious denominations that were initiated by the Second Vatican Council. Unfortunately, also, the question of amending the constitutional provisions relating to marriage and divorce became entangled in the minds of many with the issues of contraception and abortion. With churchmen fighting a rearguard action on divorce neither of the major parties was prepared to tackle this matter. By 1977, though, it was not possible to argue that it was the Church that was inhibiting change. The new Archbishop of Armagh, Dr. Tomás Ó Fiaich was, he said:

> . . . all for complete separation of Church and State.
> . . . It is good for the State and the Church . . .
>
> There would be no thundering from Armagh.
>
> On moral questions the laws of the State should be made by the legislators, and churchmen should not in any way try to bring pressure to bear on them. They might feel pressure which was not there . . .
>
> Southern politicians should have been working for the past ten years on a constitution which would be acceptable to both Protestants and Catholics.[18]

Indeed, they should have. Why, then, had they not? The answer lies in the attitude of Fianna Fáil to Articles 2 and 3. Throughout the seventies, it has been the policy of Fianna Fáil that amending those articles (which define the national territory and the applicability of the laws of the state) can be contemplated only in the context of a change in the status of Northern Ireland and as part of a negotiated settlement with Northern leaders. Kevin Boland was saying this in 1971:

> I believe there should be no changes in our present Constitution in advance of an overall settlement of the partition problem . . . Having established the essential sovereignty of a thirty-two county Ireland, we can make our own arrangements to accommodate the deep-felt aspirations of the Unionists.[19]

It was on this rock that a second all-party committee, set up in 1972 'to make recommendations on the steps now required to create conditions conducive to a United Ireland', foundered. According to Cruise O'Brien, the Fianna Fáil members of the committee,

> while declaring their willingness to go to very great lengths of concession whenever Ulster Unionists were prepared to sit around a table with the rest of us to discuss all-Ireland political arrangements, were opposed to any basic change in the absence of such a meeting.[20]

Jack Lynch, again Taoiseach, was saying the same thing at the end of 1977:

> In relation to Articles 2 and 3 . . . I adhere to the view that the time to discuss this is when elected representatives of North and South get around a table to discuss the future of the country . . .[21]

Many of the leaders of the other parties do not agree. They would be prepared to go ahead and make changes both because these are desirable in themselves and as a gesture to Northerners. A few perhaps even believe – surely against all experience? – that such gestures might be useful in getting Northern leaders 'around a table'. However, in the view of almost all of them, the absence of bi-partisan agreement on a strategy for constitutional change means that it is not possible to propose amendments relating to 'sensitive' articles. Any such proposals by the Coalition Government, in office between March 1973 and June 1977, would probably not have succeeded in a referendum in any event, and since the June 1977 general election these leaders, being in opposition, have been in no position to make proposals. Thus, in FitzGerald's words, 'we are hamstrung by Articles 2 and 3'. It is not possible, he argued, to propose major changes while retaining Articles 2 and 3. 'That could be extraordinarily damaging to our relationship with Northern Ireland': it is not possible to take them out because of Fianna Fáil inhibitions.[22] Cruise O'Brien's proposal to do this, made in January 1977 – Patrick Cooney, then Minister for Justice, made a similar proposal in September 1974 – only deepened 'the trench which divides the Coalition parties from Fianna Fáil.' It made even less likely the attainment of objectives 'which are unobtainable so long as there exists the very trench which Dr. O'Brien so vigorously and brilliantly digs.'[23]

Both Government and opposition agree that there is a need to make amendments to deal with a number of matters not connected with the Northern issue. There would probably be agreement on changes to cope with problems recently experienced in relation to bail and adoption. Changes would be needed to complete proposed university reforms. In interviews at the end of 1977, each of the party leaders identified other possible items. Lynch spoke of the possible need to amend in order to make possible 'changes in the methods of criminal investigation' and 'the proposed independent commission to draw constituency boundaries.' FitzGerald mentioned the article dealing with private property, and the antediluvian form in which the position of women is expressed. Frank Cluskey, the Labour Party leader, pointed to the need to widen the concept of the family to include one-parent families and to revise the article dealing with the right of association in the light of trade union experience.[24]

In the light of this study, one might ask whether the time has not now come for a complete overhaul. On the whole the opposition parties think it has: Jack Lynch on the other hand says that it has not:

> In general, I believe that the Constitution continues to be satisfactory both as a foundation for our institutions and system of government and as a guarantee of the rights of our citizens.[25]

Thus, in Bruce Arnold's words, 'the present prospects for serious or fundamental change are negligible.'[26] What the foregoing survey might seem to suggest is that, regardless of Northern Ireland, another stage in the evolution of the basic law of the state is now overdue, in Arnold's words, 'for the sake of the people *within* the state.'[27] There is much that is urgently needed to be done now rather than to wait upon change as a 'solution' to a problem in respect of which constitutional change in the Republic is probably peripheral.

NOTES

Introduction

1. G. M. Carter and J. H. Herz, *Government and Politics in the Twentieth Century*, 2nd ed. (London, 1965) p. 64
2. *Modern Constitutions* (London, 1966) p. 2
3. *Ibid.*, p. 3
4. Arthur N. Holcombe quoted in Harry Eckstein and David E. Apter (eds), *Comparative Politics* (Glencoe, 1963) p. 133
5. Wheare, *op. cit.*, p. 4
6. See below, p. 59

Chapter 1

1. The definitive text of the Constitution of Dáil Eireann is in Irish published in *Dáil Éireann: Minutes of the Proceedings of the First Parliament of the Republic of Ireland, 1919-21*, p. 13. Brian Farrell in 'A Note on the Dáil Constitution, 1919' in *The Irish Jurist*, vol. IV new series, pp. 127-38 (1969), gives a detailed account of the preparation of the Constitution and identifies the various drafts and translations. He shows that the original text was drafted in English and that the definitive Irish version was a translation made by Piaras Béaslaí. It is reproduced by Farrell (p. 135). Another English version, that issued to the press and published on 22 January 1919, was in turn a translation of the Irish translation (the definitive text). It is reproduced in Dorothy Macardle, *The Irish Republic*, 4th ed., pp. 923-4
2. Brian Farrell, *The Founding of Dáil Éireann: Parliament and Nation-Building* (Dublin, 1971) p. 83
3. *Ibid.*, p. 78
4. B. Farrell, *The Irish Jurist*, vol. IV, p. 135
5. See Dáil Debates, 19 June 1919, p. 131 and 17 Sept. 1920, pp. 213-14
6. B. Farrell, 'The Legislation of a "Revolutionary" Assembly: Dáil Decrees, 1919-

1922' in *The Irish Jurist,* vol. x new series, p. 116 (1975)

7. Press release by Sinn Féin, quoted in Farrell, *The Founding of Dáil Éireann,* p. 57. Farrell gives a detailed account of the preparation of the *Democratic Programme* (pp. 56-61).
8. L. Kohn, *The Constitution of the Irish Free State* (London, 1932) p. 36
9. Erhard Rumpf, *Nationalismus und Sozialismus in Irland* (Verlad Anton Hain K.G., Meisenheim am Glan, 1959) p. 43 (The translation is mine – B.C.)
10. *Michael Collins and the Making of a New Ireland* (Harrap & Co., London, 1926) vol. 1, p. 259
11. Rumpf, *op. cit.*, p. 43 (The translation is mine – B.C.)
12. B. Farrell, *The Founding of Dáil Éireann,* p. 57

Chapter 2

1. The Constitution as enacted is published in *The Constitution of the Irish Free State (Saorstát Éireann) Act, no. 1 of 1922 and the Public General Acts passed by the Oireachtas of Saorstát Éireann during the year 1922* (Stationery Office, Dublin, 1923). For accounts of the circumstances in which it was drafted and enacted see Dorothy Macardle, *The Irish Republic,* 4th ed. (Dublin, 1951); W. K. Hancock, *Survey of British Commonwealth Affairs, vol. I, Problems of Nationality, 1918-36* (London, 1937); and L. Kohn, *The Constitution of the Irish Free State* (London, 1932). Detailed studies of the work of the Constitution Committee and the drafting of the Constitution are to be found in Brian Farrell, 'The Drafting of the Irish Free State Constitution' in *The Irish Jurist,* vol. V new series, pp. 115-40 and 343-56 (1970) and vol. VI, pp. 111-35 and 345-59 (1971); and D. H. Akenson and J. F. Fallin, 'The Irish Civil War and the Drafting of the Free State Constitution' in *Éire-Ireland,* vol. V, no. 1, pp. 10-26; no. 2, pp. 42-93; no. 4, pp. 28-70 (1970).
2. Kohn, *op. cit.*, p. 103
3. *Ibid.*, p. 80
4. *Ibid.*, p. 80
5. In a memorandum submitted to the Acting Chairman of the Provisional Government, 5 August 1922, quoted in Farrell, *The Founding of Dáil Éireann,* p. 67
6. See B. Farrell, 'The Drafting of the Irish Free State Constitution' in *The Irish Jurist,* vols. V & VI, *passim.*
7. Kohn, *op. cit.*, p. 179. For the extent of the British insistence on these matters and the changes that they demanded should be made in the first draft presented by the Irish Government, see F. S. L. Lyons, 'From Free State to Republic', lecture reported in *Irish Times,* 29 August 1973.
8. Kohn, *op. cit.*, p. 179
9. F. A. Ogg, *English Government and Politics,* 2nd ed. (New York, 1936) p. 731
10. Brian Farrell, *The Irish Jurist,* vol. VI, p. 345
11. See L. Kohn, *The Constitution of the Irish Free State* (London, 1932) p. 242. The Stephens Mss. (in the Library of Trinity College, Dublin) include documents relating to a committee at work in 1925-26. The Kennedy Mss. (in the Library of University College, Dublin) include documents relating to a request to the judges for their observations and their response. (The author is grateful to Mr. Brian Farrell for drawing his attention to this material.)
12. N. Mansergh, *Survey of British Commonwealth Affairs: Problems of External Policy, 1931-1939* (London, 1952) p. 284; Chapter 8 deals with Irish policy towards the Commonwealth. In *The Restless Dominion* (London & Dublin, 1969) D. W. Harkness stresses the leading part played by the Irish in preparing the way for the Statute of Westminster.

13. N. Mansergh in F. McManus (ed.), *The Years of the Great Test* (Cork, 1967) p. 127
14. Mansergh, *Survey*, p. 289

Chapter 3

1. *Bunreacht na hÉireann (Constitution of Ireland)* (Government Publications Office, Dublin)
2. See Dáil Debates, 13 May 1937, col. 413, and 14 June, 1937, cols. 411-13. For an account of the preparation of the Constitution, see the Earl of Longford and T. P. O'Neill, *Eamon de Valera* (Dublin, 1970) pp. 290-98. See also below, p. 48. It appears to have been first drafted in English but, according to de Valera, 'the Irish drafting has gone on pari passu almost from the beginning . . . The Irish has gone side by side with that [the drafting]. We got the most competent people we could find for the Irish.' (Dáil Debates, 14 June 1937, col. 413)
3. Mansergh, *Survey, 1931-39*, p. 296
4. See V. T. H. Delany, 'The Constitution of Ireland: its Origins and Development' in *University of Toronto Law Journal*, vol. 12, pp. 7 and 8, and esp. note 44 (1957).
5. See chapter 7 below
6. The question of the appropriate name for the state arose during preparation of the draft. See Earl of Longford and T. P. O'Neill, *Eamon de Valera* (Dublin, 1970) pp. 294-5 In the draft of the Constitution originally presented to the Dáil, 'Éire' was used in both the English and the Irish texts, but during the debate Mr de Valera accepted an amendment providing for the use of the word 'Ireland' in the English text. See Dáil Debates, 25 may 1937, cols. 967-71. The Constitution is not, however, wholly consistent for in the English version of the Preamble there occur the words 'We, the people of Éire'.
7. Mansergh, *Survey, 1931-39*, p. 299
8. For a full explanation of these acts, see Mansergh, *Survey, 1931-39*, pp. 288-96.
9. Dáil Debates, 14 June 1937, col. 430
10. C. O'Leary, *The Irish Republic and its Experiment with Proportional Representation* (Notre Dame, 1961) p. 30
11. Dáil Debates, 11 May 1937, col. 60
12. No. 22 of 1948. For the circumstances leading up to this Act, see F. S. L. Lyons, *Ireland since the Famine*, rev. ed. (London, 1973) pp. 563-67. There has always been controversy about when and how the decision to repeal the External Relations Act was made despite Costello's making public an apparently authoritative account. See e.g. *Irish Times*, 7, 10, 17 & 22 January 1976.
13. See N. Mansergh (editor), *Documents and Speeches on British Commonwealth Affairs, 1931-52* (London, 1953) vol. 2, pp. 809-11.
14. Mansergh, *Survey of British Commonwealth Affairs: Problems of External Policy, 1931-1939*, p. 307
15. *Ibid.*, p. 293
16. V. T. H. Delany, 'The Constitution of Ireland: its Origin and Development' in *University of Toronto Law Journal*, vol. 12, p. 9 (1957)

Chapter 4

1. Mansergh, *Survey, 1931-1939*, p. 297. On the possible significance of the words 'derive' and 'designate' in Article 6, see G. Bowe, *The Origin of Political Authority* Dublin 1955) Chapter 8.

2. See J. H. Whyte, *Church and State in Modern Ireland,* 1923-1970 (Dublin & London, 1971) pp. 34-39
3. *Ibid.*, p. 50
4. Mansergh, *Survey,* p. 297. For a clear exposition of the view that the Constitution is firmly rooted in 'the Thomistic philosophy of the Natural Law' and is to be interpreted accordingly, see V. Grogan, 'The Constitution and the Natural Law', in *Christus Rex,* vol. 8, pp. 201-18 (1954).
5. Dáil Debates, 11 May 1937, col. 40
6. Dáil Debates, 11 May 1937, col. 51
7. Dick Walsh, Political Correspondent, *Irish Times,* 6 November 1976
8. The Offences Against the State (Amendment) Bill, 1940; the School Attendance Bill, 1942; the Electoral Amendment Bill, 1961; the Criminal Law (Jurisdiction) Bill, 1975 and the Emergency Powers Bill, 1976. In the case of the Income Tax Bill, 1966, about which the President consulted the Council of State on whether to refer, the Oireachtas passed an amending bill within the time in which the original bill could have been signed. Both bills were then signed by the President at the same time.
9. Michael McDunphy, *The President of Ireland* (Dublin, 1945) p. 52
10. D. Barrington, 'The Irish Constitution', in *Irish Monthly,* vol. 80, p. 48 (1952). For details of the composition and functions of the Council of State, see McDunphy, *op. cit.*, ch. XI.
11. See Dáil Debates, 25 May 1937, cols. 1003 ff.
12. See, e.g. the reaction to his appearance on the American television programme *Issues and Answers,* reported in *Irish Independent,* 18 July 1973.
13. For a brief account of this incident and a good discussion of the issues it raised, see M. Gallagher, 'The Presidency of the Republic of Ireland: Implications of the "Donegan Affair"' in *Parliamentary Affairs,* vol. XXX, pp. 373-84 (Autumn 1977).
14. For a brief discussion of the powers conferred on the government under Article 28.3.3° and the manner in which they have been used, see below pp. 44-5, 58-9
15. Published in the *Irish Press,* 23 October 1976.
16. *Irish Times,* 19 October 1977. For an account of the whole incident, see *Sunday Independent,* 24 October 1977. The description of Donegan is John Kelly's (Dáil Debates, 21 October 1976, col. 191.)
17. In an interview with Michael Denieffe in *Sunday Independent,* 3 July 1977
18. Dáil Debates, 21 October 1976, col. 162
19. *Irish Press,* 23 October 1976
20. Dáil Debates, 21 October 1976, col. 188. See also John Kelly's provocative article 'The garden party is over' in *Irish Times,* 25 October 1976 in which he argues that the President could answer back. As Michael Gallagher points out (*Parliamentary Affairs,* vol. XXX, pp. 380-81), the intention, expressed by de Valera in the debate on the Constitution in 1937, was otherwise.
21. *Irish Times,* 10 November 1976
22. Gallagher, *op. cit.*, p. 382

Chapter 5

1. A radical proposal for extern ministers, who were not to be members of the Oireachtas appeared in the draft of the Irish Free State Constitution. It was much modified in the constitution as enacted. Such ministers held office between

1922 and 1927. For details, see B. Chubb, *Cabinet Government in Ireland* (Dublin, 1974) pp. 23-24 and 27-28.

2. Dáil Debates, 14 June 1937, cols. 421-3
3. V. Grogan, *Administrative Tribunals in the Public Service* (Dublin, 1961) p. 7
4. For a study of the working of the cabinet system, see B. Chubb, *Cabinet Government in Ireland* (Dublin, 1974). For a more general account of Irish politics, see B. Chubb, *The Government and Politics of Ireland* (Stanford & London, 1970)
5. See p. 26 above.
6. The Constitution (Art. 51) provided that for an initial period of three years amendments could be made by the ordinary parliamentary process of legislation. Two amendments were passed in this way. Article 51 was one of the 'Transitory Provisions', for an explanation of which see p. 38 below.
7. See *More Local Government: a Programme for Development,* Report of a study group set up by the Institute of Public Administration (Dublin, 1971) and T. J. Barrington, *From Big Government to Local Government: the Road to Decentralisation* (Dublin, 1975).

Chapter 6

1. K. C. Wheare, *Modern Constitutions* (London, 1966) p. 101
2. V. T. H. Delany, 'The Constitution of Ireland: its Origins and Development' in *University of Toronto Law Journal,* vol. 12, p. 13 (1957). For a full account of the Irish judicial system see V. T. H. Delany, *The Administration of Justice in Ireland,* 4th revised edition by C. Lysaght (Dublin, 1975).
3. *Moore* v. *Attorney General for the Irish Free State* [1935] A.C. 484
4. *In re Article 28 of the Constitution and the Emergency Powers Bill, 1976* (1976) [1977] I.R. 159. See also p. 45
5. J. M. Kelly, *Fundamental Rights in the Irish Law and Constitution,* 2nd edition (Dublin, 1967) p. 14
6. D. Barrington, 'The Irish Constitution' in *Irish Monthly,* vol. 80, p. 43 (1952)
7. See B. Chubb, 'Vocational Representation and the Irish Senate' in *Political Studies,* vol. 2, pp. 97-111 (1954).
8. In F. McManus (ed), *The Years of the Great Test, 1926-39* (Cork, 1967) p. 171
9. B. Farrell 'The Drafting of the Irish Free State Constitution, III' in *The Irish Jurist,* vol. VI new series, pp. 111-112 (1971). For the text of Draft C, see *ibid.*, pp. 124-35.
10. Farrell, *op. cit.*, p. 119 and p. 111
11. Earl of Longford and T. P. O'Neill, *Eamon de Valera* (Dublin, 1970) pp. 295-6
12. D. Barrington, *op. cit.*, pp. 43-44
13. D. Costello, 'The Natural Law and The Constitution' in *Studies,* vol. 45, p. 414
14. J. M. Kelly, *Fundamental Rights in the Irish Law and Constitution,* 2nd edition (Dublin, 1967) p. 37
15. P. C. Bartholomew, *The Irish Judiciary* (Dublin, 1971) p. 53
16. Michael O'Boyle, 'Is constitutional government a luxury?' in *The Irish Times,* 10 September 1976
17. K. C. Wheare, *Modern Constitutions* (London, 1966) p. 38 and p. 42
18. O'Boyle, *op. cit.*
19. R. J. O'Hanlon, 'A Constitution for a Free People' in *Administration,* vol. 15, p. 95 (1967)

20. *In re Article 26 of the Constitution and the Emergency Powers Bill, 1976,* (1976) [1977] I.R. 159. The judgement seems to contradict the view put forward by John Kelly *Fundamental Rights in the Irish Law and Constitution,* 2nd ed. (1967) p. 21. For speculation on the possible significance of the judgement, see C. Brady, 'Emergency Powers – who will have the last say?' in *Irish Times,* 31 December 1976.
21. O'Boyle, *op cit.*
22. Kelly, *op. cit.*, pp. 57-8
23. D. Barrington, 'The Irish Constitution' in *Irish Monthly,* vol. 81, p. 49 (1953)
24. Kelly, *op. cit.*, p. 54. Lord Longford and T. P. O'Neill state that Dr. McQuaid supplied de Valera with 'paragraphs relating to private property and free competition.' based on the encyclicals *Rerum Novarum* and *Quadragesimo Anno* (*Eamon de Valera,* p. 296).
25. Wheare, *op. cit.*, p. 43
26. Kelly, *op. cit.*, p. 171-2
27. Longford and O'Neill, *op. cit.*, pp. 296-7
28. *Immortale Dei* (1885), English translation in *The Pope and The People, Select Letters and Addresses on Social Questions,* Catholic Truth Society (London, 1943) p. 48
29. *Irish Monthly,* vol. 81, p. 3
30. *Ibid.*, vol. 80, p. 380
31. 'Church and State in the Constitution of Ireland' in *The Irish Theological Quarterly,* vol. 28, p. 141 and p. 144 (1961)
32. See below, p. 67
33. But see below, p. 75
34. See V. T. H. Delany, 'The Constitution of Ireland: its Origins and Development' in *University of Toronto Law Journal,* vol. 12, p. 26. See also N. Mansergh, *Survey, 1931-39,* p. 302 and C. O'Normain 'The Influence of Irish Political Thought on the Indian Constitution' in *Indian Yearbook of International Affairs* (Madras), vol. 1, pp. 156-64 (1952).
35. R. F. V. Heuston, 'Personal Rights under the Irish Constitution', *Irish Jurist,* vol. xi(NS) 1976, p. 211. Heuston cites a number of important cases in point.
36. Dáil Debates, 9 June 1937, col. 217; for more details on de Valera's attitude to judicial review, see Kelly, *op. cit.*, pp. 17-25.
36. Dáil Debates, 3 June 1937, col. 1786

Chapter 7

1. K. Loewenstein, 'Reflections on the value of constitutions in our revolutionary age' in H. Eckstein & D. E.Apter (eds), *Comparative Politics* (Glencoe, 1963) p. 152
2. *Ibid.*, p. 154
3. Articles 52-63 were omitted from the official text of the Constitution published after June 1938. Article 51 was omitted from the official text published after June 1941.
4. In *State (Killian)* v. *The Minister for Justice* [1954] I.R. 207. See also above, pp. 38-9
5. *Acts of the Oireachtas passed in the year 1939,* Stat. Office, Dublin, pp. xi-xiii.
6. Dáil Debates, 2 Sept., 1939, col. 5
7. *Ibid.*, col. 18
8. *Ibid.*, col. 19
9. Dáil Debates, 2 April, 1941, col. 1202
10. *Ibid.*, col. 1203
11. *Ibid.*, col. 1209

12. See above, p. 45
13. McGilligan, quoted in John Kelly, *Fundamental Rights in the Irish Law and Constitution* (Dublin, 1967) p. 22; Lemass, Dáil Debates, vol. 185, col. 615 (6 December 1960); and 21 April 1964, col. 3. See also Dáil Debates of 31 August and 1 September 1976 (on emergency resolution).
14. On 17 June 1959 the electorate voted in the presidential election and on the Third Amendment of the Constitution Bill, 1958. They elected de Valera but turned down his proposal to change the voting system. See below, pp. 62-3.
15. See Dáil Debates, 7 January 1959, col. 18.
16. *Ibid.*
17. John Kelly, 'Revision of the Irish Constitution' in *Irish Times,* Monday-Wednesday, 25-27 December 1967
18. For an account of *Maria Duce* and the campaign against Article 44, see J. Whyte, *Church and State in Modern Ireland, 1923-1970* (Dublin, 1971) pp. 163-65.
19. Dáil Debates, 26 November 1958, cols. 994-997. For a full account of the debate and campaign, see G. Fitzgerald, 'P.R. – The Great Debate' in *Studies,* vol. 48, pp. 1-20 (1959).
20. Speech in Limerick on 25 March 1966, quoted in J. M. Kelly, 'Revision of the Constitution of Ireland' in *The Irish Jurist,* vol. I, new series, p. 2 (1966)
21. Dáil Debates, 31 March 1966, col. 496
22. *Report of the Committee on the Constitution, December, 1967.* Pr 9817, Stationery Office (Dublin, 1967) para. 8
23. *Ibid.*, para. 5
24. See *European Communities,* (1967), *Membership of the European Communities: Implications for Ireland* (1970); and *The Accession of Ireland to the European Communities (1972)* – all published by the Stationery Office, Dublin.
25. John Temple Lang, 'Application of the Law of the European Communities in the Republic of Ireland' in *Die Erweiterung der Europaischen Gemeinschaften,* Kölner Schriften zum Europarecht, Band 15 (Carl Heymanns Verlag KG, 1972) p. 48. For a more extended discussion of the impact of membership of the communities upon the law and the constitution, see chapter 9 below.
26. Quoted in *Irish Times,* 1 May 1972
27. Speech in Wexford, reported in *Irish Times,* 21 April 1972
28. *Irish Times,* 24 April 1972
29. *Ibid.*, 22 April 1972
30. *Ibid.*, 11 May 1972
31. Dáil Debates, 5 July 1972, col. 675
32. *Report of the Committee on the Constitution, December 1967.* Pr 9817, Stationery Office (Dublin, 1967) paras 135 and 138
33. *Ibid.*, paras 136 and 139
34. Reported in *Irish Times,* 23 September 1969
35. Dáil Debates, 2 November 1972, col. 425
36. *Ibid.*, cols. 445 and 451
37. *Ibid.*, col. 453
38. Reported in *Irish Times,* 20 November 1972
39. See e.g. *Irish Times,* 23 November and 8 December 1972.
40. Reported in *Irish Times,* 24 November 1972
41. *Irish Times,* 7 December 1972

Chapter 8

1. L. P. Beth, *The Development of Judicial Review in Ireland, 1937-1966* (Dublin, 1967) p. 1. This is the most useful work on the subject. See also E. McWhinney, *Judicial*

Review in the English-speaking World, 4th edition (Toronto, 1969) ch. 8

2. G. M. Carter and J. H. Herz, *Government and Politics in the Twentieth Century,* 2nd edition (1965) p. 78
3. Beth (*op. cit.*, p. 14) notes that on occasions lower courts have ruled on constitutional issues and he cites cases.
4. R. F. V. Heuston, 'Personal Rights under the Irish Constitution', *The Irish Jurist,* vol. XI, new series (1976), p. 209
5. See Walsh J.'s judgement in *The State (Sheerin)* v. *Kennedy* [1966] I.R. 379 at p. 388.
6 K. C. Wheare, *Modern Constitutions* (London, 1966) p. 105.
7. Heuston, *op. cit.* The quotation comes from *State (Healy)* v. *Donoghue* [1976] I.R. 325 at p. 347
8. See Wheare, *op. cit.*, pp. 106-109.
9. E. McWhinney, *Judicial Review in the English-speaking World,* 4th edition (Toronto, 1969) pp. 158 and 172.
10. L. P. Beth, *The Development of Judicial Review in Ireland, 1937-1966* (Dublin, 1967) p. 3
11. Beth, *op. cit.*, pp. 1-2
12. D. Barrington, 'Private Property under the Irish Constitution' in *The Irish Jurist,* vol. VIII new series (1973) p. 6
13. J. Kelly, *Fundamental Rights in the Irish Law and Constitution,* 2nd edition (Dublin, 1967) p. 17
14. For the period up to the middle sixties see L. P. Beth, *The Development of Judicial Review in Ireland,* 1937-1966 (Dublin, 1967); E. McWhinney, *Judicial Review in the English-speaking World,* 4th edition (Toronto, 1969); J. Kelly, *Fundamental Rights in the Irish Law and Constitution,* 2nd edition (Dublin, 1967). R. F. V. Heuston, 'Personal Rights under the Irish Constitution', also covers the period from the middle sixties to the middle seventies.
15. Beth, *op. cit.*, p. 19
16. *In re Article 26 of the Constitution and the Offences against the State (Amendment) Bill, 1940,* [1940] I.R. 470
17. McWhinney, *op. cit.*, p. 164. For examples of cases, see *In re McGrath and Harte,* [1941] I.R. and *The State (Walsh and Others)* v. *Lennon and Others,* [1942], I.R. 112
18. *Pigs Marketing Board* v. *Donnelly (Dublin) Ltd.*, [1939] I.R. 413, at p. 418
19. McWhinney, *op. cit.*, pp. 171 & 173
20. Kelly, *op. cit.*, p. 25
21. Beth, *op. cit.*, p. 45
22. [1965] I.R. 294. This case is discussed in Kelly, *op. cit.*, pp. 37-48. See also below, p. 77
23. C. McCarthy, *The Decade of Upheaval: Irish Trade Unions in the Nineteen Sixties* (Dublin, 1973)
24. See P. Bartholomew, *The Irish Judiciary* (Dublin and Notre Dame, 1971) p. 37.
25. See Kenny J.'s judgement in *Murtagh Properties Ltd.* v. *Cleary* [1972] I.R. 330 at p. 335. Heuston (*op. cit.*) also cites the following cases – *Landers* v. *Attorney General* (1975) I.L.T.R.I. and *McGee* v. *Attorney General* [1974] I.R. 284 at p. 290.
26. *In re Criminal Law (Jurisdiction) Bill 1975* (1976), 110 I.L.T.R. 69
27. Beth, *op. cit.*, p. 45
28. [1965] I.R. 294
29. [1974] I.R. 284
30. Heuston, *op. cit.*
31. *Ibid.*
32. Beth, *op. cit.*, p. 45

33. [1965] I.R. 70: [1966] I.R. 345: [1965] I.R. 70
34. Heuston, *op. cit.*
35. *Ibid.*
36. Kelly, *op. cit.*p. 47
37. McWhinney, *op. cit.*, p. 159
38. K. C. Wheare, *Modern Constitutions* (London, 1966) p. 104
39. *Ibid.*, p. 119
40. K. Loweenstein 'Reflections on the value of constitutions in our revolutionary age' in H. Eckstein and D. E. Apter (eds), *Comparative Politics* (London, 1963) p. 159

Chapter 9

1. J. Temple Lang, *The Common Market and Common Law* (Chicago and London, 1966) p. XI
2. *H. P. Bulmer Ltd.* v. *J. Bollinger S.A.* [1974] 1 ch. 401 at 418
3. Carl J. Friedrich, 'The Political Theory of the New Democratic Constitutions' in H. E. Eckstein and D. E. Apter (eds) *Comparative Politics* (Glencoe, 1963) p. 145
4. J. Temple Lang, 'Application of the Law of the European Communities in the Republic of Ireland', in *Die Erweiterung de Europäischen Gemeinschaften,* Kölner Schriften zum Europarecht, Band 15 (Carl Heymanns Verlag KG, 1972) p. 47, this book and the same author's *The Common Market and Common Law* (Chicago and London, 1966) contain authoritative discussions of the constitutional and other legal problems occasioned by Ireland's accession.
5. J. Temple Lang, 'Application of the Law of the European Communities in the Republic of Ireland', p. 48
6. 'The European Court and the European Citizen', *Euroforum,* no. 45/76, 14 December 1976 (Commission of the European Communities, Brussels) p. 6
7. J. Temple Lang, *The Common Market and Common Law,* p. 10
8. *Membership of the European Communities: Implications for Ireland,* Stationery Office (Dublin, 1970) pp. 2-4
9. *Treaty concerning the Accession of the Kingdom of Denmark, Ireland, the Kingdom of Norway and the United Kingdom to the European Economic Community [etc.],* Brussels, 22 January 1972, Stationery Office (Dublin, 1972)
10. See *55th Report of the Joint Committee on the Secondary Legislation of the European Communities,* Stationery Office (Dublin, March 1977) p. 13
11. *Membership of the European Communities: Implications for Ireland,* p. 2
12. *55th Report of the Joint Committee on the Secondary Legislation of the European Communities,* p. 9
13. See *47th Report of the Joint Committee*
14. *New Employment Legislation, 1977,* 2nd ed., Federated Union of Employers (June 1977) p. 1 (Privately circulated)
15. See *Eighteenth Annual Report of the Irish Congress of Trade Unions* (Dublin, 1976) pp. 184-91 and Appendix 7. The Congress lobbied vigorously against the Government's attempt to delay the implementation of equal pay, both in Dublin and – with some success – in Brussels.
16. C. J. Haughey, 'The Joint Committee – how it works', paper delivered to the Irish Association for European Studies seminar on the scrutiny and control of European Legislation, 23 October 1976, p. 1
17. *55th Report of the Joint Committee,* p. 9
18. Reported in *Irish Times,* 17 February 1978
19. J. Temple Lang, 'Application of the Law of the European Communities in the

Republic of Ireland', pp. 61-62. The case he refers to is reported in [1964] C.M.L.R. 425

20. 'The European Court and the European Citizen', Euroforum, no. 45/76, 14 December 1976, p. 7
21. *35th Report of the Joint Committee on the Secondary Legislation of the European Communities,* 1976, p. 9. The case referred to is case 21/74 [1974] 2 C.M.L.R. 305; see also *Defrenne* v. *Sabena,* case 43/75 [1976] C.M.L.R. 98
22. *11th Report of the Joint Committee,* 1975, p. 7. The case referred to is case 41/74 [1975] 1 C.M.L.R. 1
23. 'Fundamental Rights and the European Citizen', *Euroforum,* no. 15/77, 12 April 1977, p. 8
24. *Ibid.*, p. 7. *Handelsgesellschaft* v. *EVSt.* is case 11/70 [1972] C.M.L.R. 25. *Nold, J. K. G.* v. *E.C. Commission* is case 4/73 [1974] E.C.R. 491
25. *Membership of the European Communities: Implications for Ireland,* 1970, p. 5
26. *Ibid.*
27. Quoted *ibid.*, p. 6
28. Dennis Kennedy in *Ireland Today,* Bulletin of the Department of Foreign Affairs, no. 904 (Dublin, 15 March 1977) p. 13
29. *Fourth Report of the Government on Developments in the European Communities,* December 1974, p. 13
30. *The Common Market and the Common Law,* p. 75
31. *The Accession of Ireland to the European Communities,* Stationery Office (Dublin, 1972) p. 59

Chapter 10

1. See above, p. 21
2. C. C. O'Brien, *States of Ireland* (St. Albans, 1974) p. 116
3. Quoted in M. McInerney, '"Carrying on Fianna Fáil's Liberal Tradition": a profile of Eoin Ryan' in *Irish Times,* 12 January 1972
4. Interview by Geraldine Kennedy in a series entitled 'The Constitution 40 years on' in *Irish Times,* 29 December 1977
5. Interview by Geraldine Kennedy, *Irish Times,* 29 December 1977
6. Richie Ryan in a series entitled 'The Constitution – and the Obstacles to Unity' in *Irish Independent,* 6 December 1971
7. De Valera in a radio broadcast to the U.S.A. In 1939, quoted by C. C. O'Brien, *op. cit.*, p. 116
8. J. A. Murphy in 'The Constitution 40 years on' in *Irish Times,* 29 December 1977
9. See above, p. 22
10. J. Whyte, *Church and State in Modern Ireland* (Dublin & London, 1971) p. 334
11. *Ibid.*, p. 356
12. See above p. 64
13. G. FitzGerald, *Towards a New Ireland* (Dublin, 1973) p. 146
14. C. C. O'Brien, *States of Ireland* (London 1972) p. 293
15. G. Fitzgerald, *op. cit.*, frontispiece
16. See e.g. John Kelly, 'A Constitution for a New Ireland' in *The Irish Press* 29-31 May and 1-3 June 1972, John Temple Lang, 'A New Constitution', in *Irish Times,* 10 and 11 August 1970, The Irish Theological Association working party proposals reported in *Irish Times,* 27 May 1972
17. See above, p. 67
18. Interview quoted in *Irish Times,* 15 October 1977

19. Contribution to series entitled 'The Constitution – and the Obstacles to Unity' in *Irish Independent,* 6 December 1971
20. Quoted in *Irish Times,* 28 January 1977. For the establishment and terms of reference of the committee see Dáil Debates, vol. 260 col. 1602 (4 May 1972)
21. Interview in *Irish Times,* 29 December 1977
22. Interview in *Irish Times,* 29 December 1977
23. Bruce Arnold 'Bipartianship and the Constitution' in *Studies,* vol. LXVI, p. 7 (Spring 1977)
24. Interviews in *Irish Times,* 29 December 1977
25. *Ibid.*
26. B. Arnold, *op. cit.*, p. 1
27. *Ibid.*, p. 5. (Author's italics)

SELECT BIBLIOGRAPHY

Constitutions in General

Carl J. Friedrich, 'The Constitution as a Political Force' and 'The Political Theory of the New Democratic Constitutions' in H. E. Eckstein and D. E. Apter (eds), *Comparative Politics,* Free Press, Glencoe, 1963

K. Loewenstein, 'Reflections on the Value of Constitutions in Our Revolutionary Age' in H. E. Eckstein and D. E. Apter (eds), *Comparative Politics,* Free Press, Glencoe, 1963

K. C. Wheare, *Modern Constitutions,* 2nd ed., Oxford University Press, London, 1966

E. McWhinney, *Judicial Review in the English-Speaking World,* 4th ed., Toronto University Press, Toronto, 1969

Irish Constitutional History and Development

C. C. O'Brien, *States of Ireland,* Panther Books, St. Albans, 1974

A. G. Donaldson, *Some Comparative Aspects of Irish Law,* Duke University Press, Durham, N.C., and Cambridge University Press, London, 1957

B. Farrell, *The Founding of Dáil Éireann: Parliament and Nation Building,* Gill & Macmillan, Dublin, 1971

G. FitzGerald, *Towards a New Ireland,* Gill & Macmillan, Dublin and London, 1973

V. Grogan, 'Irish Constitutional Development' in *Studies,* vol. 40, pp. 385-98 (1951)

W. K. Hancock, *Survey of British Commonwealth Affairs, vol. 1, Problems of Nationality,* 1918-36, Oxford University Press, London, 1937

D. W. Harkness, *The Restless Dominion: The Irish Free State and the British Commonwealth of Nations,* 1921-31, Macmillan, London and Gill and Macmillan, Dublin, 1969

D. Macardle, *The Irish Republic,* 4th edition, Irish Press Ltd., Dublin, 1951

N. Mansergh, *Survey of British Commonwealth Affairs: Problems of Wartime Cooperation and Post-War Change,* 1939-52, Oxford University Press, London, 1958

D. O'Sullivan, *The Irish Free State and its Senate,* Faber & Faber, London, 1940

J. H. Whyte, *Church and State in Modern Ireland, 1923-1970,* Gill & Macmillan, Dublin & London, 1971

The Constitutions of 1919 and 1922

D. H. Akenson and J. F. Fallin, 'The Irish Civil War and the Drafting of the Free State Constitution' in *Éire-Ireland,* vol. 5, pp. 42-93 (1970)

B. Farrell, 'A Note on the Dáil Constitution, 1919', in *The Irish Jurist,* vol. IV New Series, pp. 127-38 (1969)

B. Farrell, 'The Legislation of a "Revolutionary" Assembly: Dáil Decrees, 1919-1922' in *The Irish Jurist,* vol. X New Series, pp. 112-127 (1975)

B. Farrell, 'The Drafting of the Irish Free State Constitution', *The Irish Jurist,* vol. V New Series, pp. 115-40 and 343-56 (1970) and vol. VI, pp. 111-35 and 345-59 (1971).

L. Kohn, *The Constitution of the Irish Free State,* Allen & Unwin, London, 1932

N. Mansergh, *The Irish Free State: its Government and Politics,* Allen and Unwin, London, 1934

B. Ó Briain, *The Irish Constitution,* Talbot Press, Dublin and Cork, 1929

J. G. Swift MacNeill, *Studies on the Constitution of the Irish Free State,* Dublin, 1925

Bunreacht na hÉireann

B. Arnold, 'Bipartisanship and The Constitution' in *Studies,* vol. LXVI, pp. 1-7 (1977)

D. Barrington, 'Private Property under The IrishConstitution' in *The Irish Jurist,* vol. VIII New Series, pp.1-17 1973)

D. Barrington, 'The Irish Constitution', in *Irish Monthly,* vols. 80 and 81 (twelve articles which appeared monthly between February 1952 and March 1953)

P. C. Bartholomew, *The Irish Judiciary,* Institute of Public Administration, Dublin and University of Notre Dame Press, Indiana, 1971

L. P. Beth, *The Development of Judicial Review in Ireland 1937-1966,* Institute of Public Administration, Dublin, 1967

A. W. Bromage, 'Constitutional Development in Saorstát Éireann and the Constitution of Éire' in *American Political Science Review,* vol. 31, pp. 842-61 and 1050-70 (1937)

J. P. Casey, 'The Judicial Power under Irish Constitutional Law' in *The International and Comparative Law Quarterly,* pp. 304-24 (1975)

D. Costello, 'The Natural Law and the Constitution' in *Studies,* vol. XLV, pp. 403-14 (1956)

V. T. H. Delany, 'The Constitution of Ireland, its origins and Development' in *University of Toronto Law Journal,* vol. 12, pp. 1-26 (1957)

V. T. H. Delany, 'Fundamental Liberties in the Constitution of Ireland' in *University of Malaya Law Review,* vol. 2, pp. 17-28 (1960)

M. Gallagher, 'The Presidency of the Republic of Ireland: Implications of the "Donegan Affair"' in *Parliamentary Affairs,* vol. XXX, pp. 373-84 (1977)

V. Grogan, 'The Constitution and the Natural Law', in *Christus Rex,* vol. 8, pp. 201-18 (1954)

R. F. V. Heuston, 'Personal Rights under The Irish Constitution', forthcoming in *The Irish Jurist*

J. M. Kelly, *Fundamental Rights in the Irish Law and Constitution,* 2nd ed., Allen Figgis & Co. Ltd., Dublin, 1967

J. M. Kelly, 'Revision of The Irish Constitution' in *The Irish Jurist,* vol. II New Series, p 296 (1967)

J. M. Kelly, 'A Constitution of a New Ireland' in *Irish Press,* 29-31 May and 1-3 June, 1972

E. McDonagh, 'Church and State in the Constitution of Ireland' in *The Irish Theological Quarterly,* vol. 28, pp. 131-144 (1961)

J. Newman, *Studies in Political Morality,* Scepter Press, Dublin & London, 1962 (Chapter 9 deals with the Irish political tradition and some aspects of the Constitution)

R. J. O'Hanlon, 'A Constitution for a Free People' in *Administration,* vol. 15, pp. 85-101 (1967)

A. O'Rahilly, *Thoughts on the Constitution,* Browne and Nolan, Dublin, 1937 (This pamphlet of 75 pages includes the substance of newspaper articles contributed to the *Irish Independent* and the *Catholic Herald*)

J. Temple Lang, 'Application of the Law of the European Communities in the Republic of Ireland', in *Die Erweiterung der Europäischen Gemeinschaften, Kölner Schriften zum Europarecht, Band 15, Carl Heymanns Verlag KG, 1972*

Report of The Committee on the Constitution, December, 1967, Stationery Office Dublin, 1967

'The Constitution – and The Obstacles to Unity', in *Irish Independent,* 6 December 1971

'The Constitution 40 Years On', in *Irish Times,* 29 and 30 December 1977 (A series of intervies by Geraldine Kelly. Interviewees included Jack Lynch, Garret FitzGerald, Frank Cluskey, John A. Murphy.)

LIST OF CONSTITUTIONAL ARTICLES

INDEX

This Index was prepared by Brigid Pike.